The Wit & Wisdom of
The Art of the Put-Down

First Published in Great Britain in 2006 by
House of Raven Book Services
King's Sutton
OX17 3RS

Typeset in Mylius Sans and ITC Officina Serif
Design, and illustration: David Coventon
Additional design: Bradley Hotson & Patrik Hartmann
Additional illustration: Sarah Raven

Printed in China by Imago

ISBN: 1905403054

The Wit & Wisdom of
The Art of the Put-Down

Compiled and Edited by Nick Holt

Haven't we all longed for that mot-juste when on the receiving end of an ear-bashing from a customer or client or colleague?

Haven't we all struggled for the right phrase when describing the inhuman inadequacy of our friends, our football team or the entire human race?

Haven't we all ached for the pithy one-liner to shrink the guy in the Porsche looking smug at the traffic lights?

Haven't we all dreamed of writing the ultimate scathing review of the piece of unspeakable garbage we were made to sit through at the cinema?

If this is you, then here is the answer to your prayers.

CONTENTS

There are over 1,200 quotes in this collection. Each quote that appears is numbered (i.e. ·123). These numbers run sequentially throughout the book. Use the index at the back to find great exponents of the put-down. The index is listed in alphabetical order by surname.

*For Martin, for always
laughing at my gags*

GET HER!

If you haven't got anything good to say about anyone come and sit by me.

Alice Roosevelt Longworth had this maxim embroidered upon a cushion; in Michael Teague, *Mrs L: Conversations with Alice Roosevelt Longworth* (1981) ·1

Judge: *You are extremely offensive, young man.*

Smith: *As a matter of fact, we both are, and the only difference between us is that I am trying to be, and you can't help it.*

Conservative politician and lawyer F.E. Smith,
Lord Birkenhead; Earl of Birkenhead (1933) ·2

I hope all your children have very small dicks! And that includes the girls!

Jeff Goldblum as Dexter
in *The Tall Guy* (1989) ·4

I fart in your general direction! Your mother was a hamster and your father smells of elderberries.

Insulting French soldier in *Monty Python
sand The Holy Grail* (1975) ·3

May she marry a ghost, and bear him a kitten, and may the High King of Glory permit it to get the mange.

James Stephens ·5

You are all camphire and frankincense, all chastity and odour.

William Congreve, *The Way of the World* (1700) ·6

I regard you with an indifference closely bordering on aversion.

Robert Louis Stevenson, *New Arabian Nights* (1882) ·7

Because thou art lukewarm and neither cold nor hot, I will spue thee out of my mouth.

Bible, Revelation 3.16 ·8

Some men are born mediocre, some men achieve mediocrity, and some men have mediocrity thrust upon them, With Major Major it has been all three.

Joseph Heller, *Catch-22* (1961) ·9

He really is terribly heavy going. Like running up a hill in roller skates.

Alan Ayckbourn, from *Living Together* (1975) ·10

The only gracious way to accept an insult is to ignore it; if you can't ignore it, top it; if you can't top it, laugh at it; if you can't laugh at it, it's probably deserved.

Russell Lynes, American writer and critic ·11

If I throw a stick, will you leave?

Anon. ·12

He waltzes like a Protestant curate.

Kate O'Brien, from *The Last of Summer* (1943) ·13

One more push, I'm gonna to smack his face so hard he'll have to stick his toothbrush up his arse to clean his teeth!

Terence Stamp as Bernadette in *Adventures of Priscilla, Queen of the Desert* (1994) ·14

I wouldn't piss in his ear if his brain was on fire.

Quoted by Bill Clinton as a traditional expression of dislike in the Southern United States; in *My Life* (2004) ·15

Let him be damned in his going and coming in. The Lord strike him with madness and blindness. May the heavens empty upon him thunderbolts and the wrath of the Omnipotent burn itself unto him in the present and future world. May the Universe light against him and the earth open to swallow him up.

Pope Clement VI (1478-1534) invokes a happy prospect for excommunicated sinners. ·16

One should forgive one's enemies, but not before they are hanged.

Heinrich Heine [17]

Nothing trivial, I hope.

John Pentland Mahaffy, on hearing of the illness of Traill who in 1904 had beaten him to the Provostship of Trinity Dublin; Ulick O'Connor, *Oliver St John Gogarty* (1964) [18]

There is no sin except stupidity.

Oscar Wilde, *'The Critic as Artist'* (1891) [19]

'I am inclined to think — said I' [Dr Watson]. 'I should do so,' Sherlock Holmes remarked, impatiently.

Arthur Conan Doyle, *The Valley of Fear* (1915) [20]

Clevinger was one of those people with lots of intelligence and no brains, and everyone knew it except those who soon found it out. In short, he was a dope.

Joseph Heller, *Catch-22* (1961) [21]

Mr Kremlin himself was distinguished for ignorance, for he had only one idea, — and that was wrong.

Benjamin Disraeli, *Sybil* (1845) ·22

I don't think there's intelligent life on other planets. Why should other planets be any different from this one?

Bob Monkhouse, attrib., in BBC News December 2003 **(online ed.)** ·23

The march of the human mind is slow.

Edmund Burke ·24

We've all heard that a million monkeys banging on a million typewriters will eventually reproduce the entire works of Shakespeare. Now, thanks to the Internet, we know this is not true.

Robert Wilensky, in *Mail on Sunday* February 1997 ·25

You beat your pate, and fancy wit will come: Knock as you please, there's nobody at home.

Alexander Pope, *'Epigram: You beat your pate'* (1732) ·26

He may look an idiot and talk like an idiot but don't let that fool you. He really is an idiot.

Groucho Marx ·27

Oh dear, why does Lydia always come in — and why must she beg me to believe that she thinks seriously every day of her life, as she says? When her brain is a cage of canaries?

Virginia Woolf on the Russian ballerina Lydia Lopokova ·28

I always like to compare models to supermodels in the way I compare Tampax to SuperTampax: supermodels cost a bit more and they are a lot thicker.

Jo Brand ·29

Squire: *If I had a son who was an idiot, by Jove, I'd make him a parson!*

Sydney Smith: *Very probably, but I see that your father was of a different mind.*

The Rev. Sydney Smith, wit, essayist and canon of St. Paul's Cathedral. ·30

To call you stupid would be an insult to stupid people. I've known sheep that could outwit you; I've worn dresses with higher IQs. But you think you're an intellectual, don't you, ape?

Jamie Lee Curtis as Wanda in *A Fish Called Wanda* (1988) ·31

You couldn't pour piss out of a boot if the instructions were on the heel.

Lyndon Baines Johnson to a subordinate; in *Robert Caro, The Years of Lyndon Johnson: Master of the Senate* ·32

I never forget a face, but in your case I'll be glad to make an exception.

Groucho Marx; in *Leo Rosten, People I have Loved, Known or Admired* (1970), *'Groucho'* ·33

He had the sort of face that makes you realise God does have a sense of humour.

Bill Bryson, *Neither Here Nor There* (1991) ·35

Is that your face, or has your head just vomited?

Comedian Julian Clary deals with hecklers ·34

My face looks like a wedding cake that has been left out in the rain.

W. H. Auden on himself ·36

Were a fly to attempt to cross it, it would break its leg.

Lord David Cecil on the heavily wrinkled face of W.H. Auden, described by the poet himself as like a wedding cake left out in the rain; in *A.L.Rowse diary*, 30 May 1960 ·37

I kept thinking, if his face was that wrinkled, what did his balls look like?

David Hockney ponders the important questions after drawing W.H. Auden; attrib. ·38

We had the old Crow over at Hull recently, looking like a Christmas present from Easter Island.

Philip Larkin, of fellow poet Ted Hughes; *letter*, 1975 ·39

Twin miracles of mascara, her eyes looked like the corpses of two small crows that had crashed into a chalk cliff.

Clive James on a TV interview with Barbara Cartland, in the *Observer*, August 1981 ·40

Topaz was wonderfully patient — but I sometimes wonder if it is not only patience, but also a faint resemblance to cows.

Dodie Smith ·41

Why did he [Onassis] marry that Jackie? She is ugly, with horrible legs, the skin of a hen, fat in the wrong places, and eyes too far apart from one another. She's a big nothing.

Aristotle Onassis finds a formidable opponent in Lisa Calogeropoulos, mother of his former mistress Maria Callas. ·42

She's what I call a 'two bagger' — you have to put a bag over her head and one over your own head in case hers breaks.

Mark Lamarr ·44

My face looks like a bouquet of elbows.

American comedian Phyllis Diller ·43

If I had a head like yours, I'd have it circumcised.

Dave Allen, comedian, quoted in *The Times Book of Quotations* ·45

A cherub's face, a reptile all the rest.

Alexander Pope, of Lord Hervey;
'An Epistle to Doctor Arbuthnot' (1735) •46

He looked like Rameses II with his wrappings off.

Hugh Fullerton •47

A red-haired, red-faced, man of 65 seemingly in transit between Dr Jekyll and Mr Hyde.

Peter McKay on Pal Johnson,
in **the Sunday Times**,
November 1993 •48

He looked like an extra from a crowd by Hieronymus Bosch.

Kenneth Tynan •49

He was there with two very worn and chipped looking ladies — the saddest looking remnants of ladies — in fact they reminded me of those cups without saucers that you sometimes see outside a china shop — all-on-this-tray-one-penny.

Katherine Mansfield ·50

At least, she is not any worse-looking than she used to be in her youth; hers are features which never alter, unfortunately for her.

George Sand ·51

*[He looks like]
an explosion in a
pubic hair factory.*

Jonathan Miller, of British journalist Paul
Johnson; in *Alan Watkins, Brief Lives* (1982) ·52

*Never trust
a man who
combs his hair
straight from
his left armpit.*

Alice Roosevelt Longworth on *'the careful
distribution of hair on General MacArthur's
balding head';* Michael Teague, *Mrs L:
Conversations with Alice Roosevelt
Longworth* (1981) ·53

*Two bursts
in a sofa.*

Bobby Corbett describes the particularly
hirsute armpits of a Wimbledon spectator;
recalled in his obituary, *Daily Telegraph*
13 March 1999 ·54

She looks like she combs her hair with an egg-beater.

Louella Parsons on Joan Collins ·55

Why don't you get a haircut? You look like a chrysanthemum.

P.G. Wodehouse ·56

You can have affection for a murderer or a sodomite, but you cannot have affection for a man whose breath stinks.

George Orwell ·57

My Grandmother took a bath every year, whether she needed it or not.

Bernard Behan ·58

She looked like Lady Chatterley above the waist and the gamekeeper below.

Cyril Connolly, on Vita Sackville-West ·59

You have sent me a Flanders mare.

Henry VIII when he saw Anne of Cleves, his fourth wide, for the first time quoted by Tobias Smollett ·61

This Englishwoman is so refined
She has no bosom and no behind.

Stevie Smith,
'This Englishwoman'
(1937) ·60

Hester bobbed up again as usual, grown fat and blowsy with ankles that look like the thick end of asparagus.

Virginia Woolf ·62

Her figure is corpulent, her complexion coarse, one eye gone, and her neck immense.

Lady Holland, on Lady Georgiana Spencer ·63

She fitted into my biggest armchair as if it had been built around her by someone who knew they were wearing armchairs tight about the hips that season.

P.G. Wodehouse, *My Man Jeeves* (1919) ·64

I'd kill myself if I was that fat.

Elizabeth Hurley ponders the charm of Marilyn Monroe. ·65

*I cannot believe the size of her butt. If she does appear in **Playboy**, it will have to be an extra big edition*

Joan Collins on Monica Lewinsky. ·66

A man explained inflation to his wife thus: 'When we married you measured 36-24-36. Now you're 42-42-42. There's more of you, but you're not worth as much.' Joel Barnett, attrib.; in *Mail on Sunday,* October 2003 ·67

She had very thick ankles.

Thomas Griffiths Wainewright's justification for poisoning his sister-in-law; in *Dictionary of National Biography* (1917) ·69

In response to her husband's question regarding the age of a particularly thick-limbed starlet: For God's sake, Walter, why don't you chop off her legs and read the rings?

Carol Matthau; in *Truman Capote, Answered Prayers* (1986) ·68

He was so fat if he sat on a worm on a rock it would make a fossil in about five minutes. Then scientists wouldn't have to wait a million years.

Jane Hamilton ·70

Lord Northcliffe: *The trouble with you, Shaw, is that you look as if there were a famine in the land.*
Shaw: *The trouble with you, Northcliffe, is that you look as if you were the cause of it.*

Playwright George Bernard Shaw, in an exchange with portly newspaper tycoon Lord Northcliffe (Alfred Charles William Harmsworth, 1865-1922) •71

In a New York bath house, where the practice for those wanting a partner was to leave the cubicle door open, a young man recoiled on seeing John Schlesinger's 'mound of flesh':
Anonymous: *Oh, please. I couldn't. You've got to be kidding.*
Schlesinger: *A simple 'No' will suffice.*

John Schlesinger, in *Alan Bennett, diary 2003;* in *London Review of Books* January 2004 •72

Naked, I had a body that invited burial.

Spike Milligan ·73

My genitals are like a sort of travel version of Linford Christie's.

Frank Skinner ·74

My best birth control now is to leave the lights on.

American comedienne Joan Rivers ·75

Well, Nell, said she, presenting her cool peach cheek to me, how are you? Much the same as usual I see — hair arranged with a pitchfork and dress with a view to ventilation.

Rhoda Broughton ·76

She wears her clothes as if they were thrown on her with a pitchfork.

Jonathan Swift, *Polite Conversation* (1738) •77

Victoria Beckham gives away all her old clothes to starving children. Well who else are they going to fit?

Pauline Calf •78

Jordan doesn't need a fashion designer. She needs a structural engineer. **Frank Skinner** •79

Like a fist fight in a hydrangea bush.

Craig Brown on buxom Dame Jill Knight wearing a floral print •80

Englishwomen's shoes look as if they had been made by someone who had often heard shoes described, but had never seen any.

Margaret Halsey, 1938 •81

Miss Strozzi… had the temerity to wear as truly horrible a gown as I have ever seen on the American stage. There was a flowing skirt of pale chiffon — you men don't have to listen — and a bodice of rose-coloured taffeta, the sleeves of which extended shortly below her shoulders. Then there was an expanse of naked arms, and then, around the wrists, taffeta frills such as are fastened about the unfortunate necks of beatend white poodle-dogs in animal acts. Had she not luckily been strangled by a member of the cast while disporting this garment, I should have fought my way to the stage and done her in myself.

Dorothy Parker reviews *Kay Strozzi* in *The Silent Witness*, in *The New Yorker*, 1931 ·82

A brilliant blue garment that was an offence alike to her convictions and her complexion.

Edith Somerville and Martin Ross, *Further Experiences of an Irish R.M.* (1908) ·83

Perhaps the Majors and the Blairs and all the power-dressers of Britain should take the advice of Wallis Simpson to the Queen Mother who, when asked how she could best promote British fashion abroad, replied crisply: Stay at home.

From *The Wit and Wisdom of the Royal Family* ·84

She made her look like a lampshade in a curry house.

Journalist Andrew Marr responds to reports that 'style guru' Carole Caplin was responsible for dressing President Putin's wife for the Russian state visit; in *Daily Telegraph* July 2003 *(online ed.)* •85

The Pope. Great guy. But in a fashion sense, he's one hat away from being the Grand Wizard of the Ku Klux Klan.

Jon Stewart •87

Now I know the meaning of the word 'grotesque'.

Sydney Smith, on seeing Mrs Grote in a huge rose-coloured turban; Peter Virgin, *Sydney Smith* (1994) •86

Christian Dior's New Look consists of clothes by a man who doesn't know women, never had one, and dreams of being one. Coco Chanel ·88

In appearance Dior is like a bland country curate made out of pink marzipan.

Cecil Beaton describes legendary couturier
Christian Dior; *The Glass of Fashion* (1954) ·89

Noël Coward (to Edna Ferber, who was wearing a tailored suit):
You look almost like a man.
Edna Ferber: So do you.

Coward ·90

When a woman looks at a man in evening dress, she sometimes can't help wondering why he wants to blazon his ancestry to the world by wearing a coat with a long tail to it.
Helen Rowland ·91

One thing I've learned from both **Star Trek** *and* **Moonbase** *is that men are going to be wearing simple pullovers for ever. I never did think that all that shoulder padding forecast by Hollywood in its science fiction would really catch on. I've also learned, not to my surprise, that women will continue to sport minis and plenty of décolletage whatever the stardate.*

Bernard Hollowood in *Punch,* September 1973 ·92

MUTUAL INCOMPATIBILITY

*Until Eve gave him the apple,
[Adam] didn't even know he
wasn't wearing underpants.*

Paula Yates ·93

Nature intended women to be our slaves… they are our property; we are not theirs. They belong to us, just as a tree that bears fruit belongs to a gardener. What a mad idea to demand equality for women!… Women are nothing but machines for producing children.

Napoleon Bonaparte •94

Nature, I say, doth paynt them further to be weak, fraile, impacient, feble, and foolishe; and experience hath declared them to be unconstant, variable, cruell, and lacking in the spirit of counsel and regiment.

John Knox, *The First Blast of the Trumpet Against the Monstrous Regiment of Women* (1558) •95

A woman without a man is like a fish without a bicycle.

Gloria Steinem; attrib. •96

The 'g' is silent. The only thing about her that is.

Journalist Julie Burchill on self-styled feminist bisexual egomaniac Camille Paglia; in *The Spectator,* 1992 •97

All this Women's Liberation noise, I'm for it, of course — what I'm against is their idea that they invented it.

Katherine Hepburn •98

Whatever women do they must do twice as well as men to be thought half as good. Luckily, this is not difficult.

Charlotte Whitton (1896-1975), **former mayor of Ottowa.** •99

Well, I've finally figured out that being male is the same thing, more or less, as having a personality disorder.

Carol Shields ·100

Dullards, malingerers, gigolos, sycophants, boors — and that's the best of them… betrayers all. None of them worth the socks they stick their big feet into.

American novelist Lucy Ellmann ·102

Maleness remains a recessive genetic trait like colour—blindness and haemophilia.

Elizabeth Gould Davies ·101

How often the Gods endow a man with a perfect profile and no brains to live up to it.

Katherine Mansfield ·103

I think men are very funny. If I had one of those dangly things stuffed down the front of my pants, I'd sit at home all day laughing at myself.

Dawn French ·104

Are you my alternative?

Florynce R. Kennedy responds to a heckler who asked if she was a lesbian. ·106

Men can read maps better than women. 'Cos only the male mind could conceive of one inch equalling a hundred miles.

Roseanne Barr ·105

Not tonight, Josephine.

Napoleon I; attrib. but probably apocryphal; Ned Sherrin cites R.wH. Horne, *The History of Napoleon,* as describing the circumstances in which the notorious affront might have occurred. ·107

[Some guys] make love like they were the only ones in the room, which I think is a holdover from when they were.

Diane Nichols ·108

He had ambitions, at one time, to become a sex maniac, but he failed his practical.

British comic Les Dawson; attrib. ·109

Like having a large wardrobe fall on top of you with the key still in the lock.

A former girlfriend's description of being made love to by Nicholas Soames; in Gyles Brandreth, *Breaking the Code* (1999) ·110

Roseanne went on Saturday Night Live and said I had a 3-inch penis. Well, even a 747 looks small if it's landing in the Grand Canyon.

Tom Arnold ·111

You were born with your legs apart. They'll send you to the grave in a Y—shaped coffin.

Joe Orton, *What the Butler Saw* (1969) ·112

Remember, you're fighting for this woman's honour, which is probably more than she ever did.

Groucho Marx as Firefly in *Duck Soup*(1933) ·113

She has been kissed as often as a police-court Bible, and by much the same class of people.

Robertson Davies ·115

*Here lies all that
  remains of Charlotte,
Born a virgin, died
  a harlot.
For sixteen years she
  kept her virginity,
A marvellous thing for
  this vicinity.*

Anonymous epitaph found in Welland, Ont. ·114

She's had more hands up her dress than the Muppets.

Joan Rivers on her fictional character, Heidi Abromowitz •117

Lulubelle, it's you! I didn't recognise you standing up.

Groucho Marx as S Quentin Quale in *Go West* (1940) •116

Her legs were apart so often they were pen pals.

Joan Rivers embellishes the reputation of her fictional character Heidi Abromowitz •118

There, standing at the piano, was the original good time who had been had by all.

Kenneth Tynan, while an undergraduate, at an Oxford Union debate; (also attributed to Bette Davies of a passing starlet) ·119

The t is silent, as in Harlow.

Margot Asquith corrects Jean Harlow and hints at her reputation) after the actress had mispronounced her first name; in T.S. Matthews, *Great Tom* (1973) ·120

She sleeps alone at last.

Suggested epitaph for an unnamed movie queen with a notoriously active love-life; Robert Benchley, attrib. ·121

We have a BBC safety hazards form that we fill in before any production, but being kissed by Christine Hamilton didn't come into that unfortunately.

Louis Theroux, who made a documentary on disgraced Tory MP Neil Hamilton and his formidable wife. ·122

A lot of men get very funny about women drinking: they don't really like it. Well, I'm sorry lads, but if we didn't get pissed, most of you would never get a shag.

Jenny Eclair ·123

Steff: I've been out with a lot of girls at this school. I don't see what makes you so different.

Andie: I have some taste.

James Spader and Molly Ringwald in *Pretty In Pink* (1986) ·124

Save your breath! You'll need it to inflate your girlfriend!

Anon. ·125

Cher: I want to do something good for humanity.

Josh: Try sterilisation.

Alicia Silverstone and Paul Rudd in *Clueless* (1995) ·126

Friend: Member of the opposite sex in your acquaintance who has some flaw which makes sleeping with him/her totally unappealing.

The Dictionary of Dating ·127

On refusing to allow his biographer Sheridan Morley to reveal his homosexuality, despite the recent 'outing' of theatre critic T.C. Worsley: You forget that the great British public would not care if Cuthbert Worsley had slept with mice.

Noël Coward; in *Independent on Sunday magazine,* November 1995 ·128

Believing that his hate for queers
Proclaimed his love for God,
He now (of all queer things, my dears)
Lies under his first sod.

Paul Dehn, on *Sunday Express* **editor John Gordon** (1890-1974); **in Nigel Rees,** *Cassell Dictionary of Humorous Quotations* (1999) ·129

Marriage, n. The state or condition of a community consisting of a master, a mistress and two slaves, making in all, two.

Ambrose Bierce, *The Devil's Dictionary* (1911) •130

In Church your grandsire
  cut his throat;
To do the job too long
  he tarry'd,
He should have had my
  hearty vote,
To cut his throat before
  he marry'd.

Jonathan Swift, *Verses On The Upright Judge* (1724) •131

Marry me, and I'll never look at any other horse.

Groucho Marx as Hackenbush in *A Day at the Races* (1937) •132

I have always thought that every woman should marry, and no man.

Benjamin Disraeli •133

The trouble with some women is that they get all excited about nothing — and then they marry him.

Cher •134

Marriage makes an end of many short follies — being one long stupidity.

Friedrich Nietzsche •135

A TV host asked my wife, 'Have you ever considered divorce?' She replied: 'Divorce never, murder often.'

Charlton Heston; in *Independent*
July 1999 ·136

I'm sure Mick Jagger will find someone else to be unfaithful to soon. Jerry Hall ·137

There was a time when those in public life attempted to behave with discretion and not like a stray mongrel in a public park.

Lord Cobham, whose wife left him for former Conservative Cabinet Minister David Mellor. ·138

Lady Carina Fitzalan-Howard, on being asked if her future husband David Frost was religious:
Yes, he thinks he's God Almighty.

Carina Frost; in *Sunday Times*,
July 1985 •139

*Ye stupid auld bitch —
I beg your pardon, I
mistook ye for my wife.*

Lord Braxfield (1722-99) shouts at his whist
partner; attrib., quoted in *Literary Review*,
November 2003 •141

*A man should not insult
his wife publicly, at parties.
He should insult her in
the privacy of the home.*

James Thurber, from *Thurber Country*
(1953) •140

Mrs Teasdale:
My husband is dead.
*Firefly: I'll bet he's just
using that as an excuse.*
*Mrs Teasdale: I was
with him to the end.*
*Firefly: No wonder he
passed away.*
*Mrs Teasdale: I held him
in my arms and kissed him.*
Firefly: So it was murder!

Margaret Dumont and Groucho
in *Duck Soup* (1933) ·142

*A man… is so in
the way in the house!*

Elizabeth Gaskell, *Cranford* (1853) ·143

*The comfortable estate
of widowhood, is the
only hope to keep
up a wife's spirits.*

John Gay, *The Beggar's Opera* (1728) ·144

Admiral Roebuck (Geoffrey Palmer): With all due respect M, I don't think you have the balls for this.

M (Judi Dench): Perhaps. The advantage is I don't have to think with them all the time.

Exchange from *Tomorrow Never Dies* (1997) with the woman on top — a rare moment in a *Bond* movie. ·145

(IM)POLITE SOCIETY

...Hell is other people.

Jean-Paul Sartre, *Huis Clos,* (1944) •146

I have my bitchy side, but I don't think I'm really nasty. I think that a lot of other people probably think that I am. Fuck them.

Blondie front-woman Debbie Harry ·147

I am very sorry to hear that Duff [Cooper] is surprised and grieved to hear that I had detested him for 23 years. I must have nicer manners than people normally credit me with.

Evelyn Waugh, letter to Lady Diana Cooper, 29 August 1953 ·148

She proceeds to dip her little fountain-pen filler into pots of oily venom and to squirt this mixture at all her friends.

Harold Nicolson, of the society hostess Mrs Ronnie Greville; *diary,* 20 July 1937 ·149

She really is very close to a charming character; if she had had the small pox she would have been so.

Mrs Gaskell on Effie Gray, John Ruskin's wife. ·150

I cannot compassionate the countess, since I think her insolent character deserves all the mortifications Heaven can send her.

Lady Mary Wortley Montagu ·151

Neighbours. I'd rather have thrush.
Pamela Stephenson ·152

I have got several very bad new lunatics, most of them religious, and some just ordinary housewives, who try to write a little.

Edith Sitwell on the guests at a forthcoming dinner party at her house. ·153

I must go and see what that poor gaping imbecile my charwoman is doing about dinner.

Virginia Woolf ·154

Dinner at the Hunterscombes' possessed 'only two dramatic features — the wine was a farce and the food a tragedy'.

Anthony Powell, *The Acceptance World* (1955) ·155

When he has a party, you not only bring your own scotch, you bring your own rocks.

George Burns on Jack Benny ·156

Very sorry can't come. Lie follows by post.

Baron Beresford replying to an invitation to dinner from Edward Prince of Wales ·157

I've had a perfectly wonderful evening, but this wasn't it.

Groucho Marx ·158

Bore, n. A person who talks when you wish him to listen.

Ambrose Bierce ·159

At a party one evening the painter James McNeill Whistler found himself cornered by a notorious bore. "You know, Mr Whistler," the bore said, "I passed your house last night." "Thank you", Whistler replied.

Whistler ·160

He is not only dull in himself, but the cause of dullness in others.

Samuel Foote, on a dull lord, in Boswell's
Life of Samuel Johnson (1791) 1783 ·161

Underneath this flabby exterior is an enormous lack of character.

Oscar Levant, *Memoirs of an Amnesiac* (1965) ·162

A Merry Christmas to all my friends except two.

W.C. Fields, attrib. ·165

I've tried him drunk and I've tried him sober but there's nothing in him.

Charles II (1630-85), of his niece Anne's husband George of Denmark, in Guila Curtis, *The Life and Times of Queen Anne* (1972) ·163

Champagne for my real friends, and real pain for my sham friends.

Francis Bacon (1909-92) makes his favourite toast; Michael Peppiatt, *Francis Bacon* (1996) ·164

You and I were long friends; you are now my enemy, and I am Yours, B. Franklin

Benjamin Franklin, *letter to William Strahan* ·166

Cicely: *When I see a spade, I call it a spade.*
Gwendolen: *I am glad to say that I have never seen a spade. It is obvious that our social spheres have been widely different.*

Oscar Wilde, *The Importance of Being Earnest* (1895) Act III •167

Grandmother used to take my mother to the circus to see the fat lady and tattooed man. Now they're everywhere.

Joan Collins •168

The truckman, the trashman and the policeman on the block may call me Alice but you may not.

Alice Roosevelt Longworth to Senator Joseph McCarthy; in Michael Teague, *Mrs L: Conversations with Alice Roosevelt Longworth* (1981) •169

Egotism — usually just a case of mistaken nonentity.

Barbara Stanwyck, American actress. ·170

He was like a cock who thought the sun had risen to hear him crow.

George Eliott, *Adam Bede,* (1859) ·171

Blessed are the famous, for they will enjoy the praise of men.

The Archbishop of Canterbury satirises modern values ·172

Repartee, n.
Prudent insult in retort.
Practiced by gentlemen
with a constitutional
aversion to violence,
but a strong disposition
to offend. Ambrose Bierce,
The Devil's Dictionary
(1911) •173

If you say a modern
celebrity is an adulterer, a
pervert and a drug addict,
all it means is that you've
read his autobiography.

P.J. O'Rourke, **Give War a Chance** (1992) •175

You can file Madonna's quote
in the dictionary of clichés
under 'pot and kettle'.

Ben Affleck responds to Madonna's reported
accusation that he and Jennifer Lopez had
courted media attention. •174

Ali G interviewing David and
Victoria Beckham: *So they is*
some people who suddenly get
loads of money who become
very tasteless. How has you
two managed to avoid that?

Ali G (Sacha Baron Cohen); in **Sunday Times**
February 2001 •176

We invite people like that to tea, but we don't marry them.

Lady Chetwode on her future son-in-law, John Betjeman ·177

There is very little pure blood left in this country, as most of it is tainted with cocaine.

Jenny Eclair on the English upper classes ·179

I can't see the sense in it really. It makes me a Commander of the British Empire. They might as well make me a Commander of Milton Keynes — at least that exists.

Spike Milligan on the 'honour' of being made a CBE in 1992; attrib., *Daily Telegraph* February 2002 ·178

Aristo-prats always use the fact that their parents didn't love them to go round causing havoc. No wonder their parents didn't love them, the nasty little gutless inbreds.

Jenny Eclair ·180

The institution of monarchy is inherently silly.

Lord Hattersley. ·181

Henry VIII, or King Syphilis Gut Bucket Wife Murderer VIII as I prefer to call him, was born in 1491. Jo Brand ·182

Eulogy, n. Praise of a person who has either the advantages of wealth and power, or the consideration to be dead.

Ambrose Bierce, *The Devil's Dictionary* (1911) ·183

Here lies a great and mighty king Whose promise none relies on; He never said a foolish thing Nor ever did a wise one.

John Wilmot, Earl of Rochester composes *'The King's Epitaph* for reigning monarch Charles II ·184

This is very true: for my words are my own, and my actions are my ministers'.

Charles II's response to Rochester's epitaph; in Thomas Hearne: *Remarks and Collections* (1885-1921) ·185

Who's your fat friend?

George 'Beau' Brummel, to Beau Nash as the latter appeared accompanied by the Prince Regent, later George IV ·186

A more contemptible, cowardly, selfish, unfeeling dog does not exist than this King… with vices and weakness of the lowest and most contemptible order.

Charles Greville, diarist, on George IV ·187

Most Gracious Queen,
  we thee implore
To go away and sin no more,
But if that effort be too great,
To go away at any rate.

Anonymous; epigram on Queen Caroline (Caroline of Brunswick), unpopular wife of George IV, quoted in a *letter from Francis Burton to Lord Colchester*, November 1820 ·188

The King blew his nose twice, and wiped the royal perspiration repeatedly from a face which is probably the largest uncivilised spot in England.

Oliver Wendell Holmes on British monarch William IV. ·189

For seventeen years George V did nothing at all but kill animals and stick in stamps.

Harold Nicholson ·190

It's most unfortunate that all my sons have such long eyelashes while my daughter hasn't any at all.

The Queen on Princess Anne (and co.) ·191

Such an attractive lass. So outdoorsy. She loves nature in spite of what it did to her.

Bette Midler on Princess Anne. ·192

Of all the Royals, Anne is the rudest. If anyone crosses her, she lays back her ears, bares her teeth, and kicks them to splinters.

Jean Rook ·193

She is a lady short on looks, absolutely deprived of any dress sense, has a figure like a Jurassic monster (seems) very greedy when it comes to loot, tact and wants to upstage everyone else.

Sir Nicholas Fairburn on Sarah, the Duchess of York, in the *Independent.* ·194

I couldn't believe it when I picked up a newspaper and read that 82 per cent of men would rather sleep with a goat than me.

Sarah Ferguson ·195

Shea was a master of evasion, more slippery than a Jacuzzi full of KY Jelly.

Richard Littlejohn on Michael Shea, the Queen's former press secretary, in *The Sun* ·196

If one were going to be interviewed by anyone, it wouldn't be you.

The Queen shows John Humphrys of Radio 4's *Today* **programme that she too has mastered that art of the put-down** ·197

Prince Charles is an insensitive, hypocritical oaf and Princess Diana is a selfish, empty-headed bimbo. They should never have got married in the first place. I blame the parents

Richard Littlejohn, in *The Sun* ·198

I cannot but conclude the bulk of your natives to be the most pernicious race of little odious vermin that nature ever suffered to crawl upon the surface of the earth.

Jonathan Swift, *Gulliver's Travels* (1726)
'A Voyage to Brobdingnag' ·199

Why cannot you go down to Bristol and see some of the third and forth class people there, and they'll do just as well?

Lady Holland to Charles Dickens, on hearing of his proposed trip to America; in U. Pope-Hennessy, *Charles Dickens* (1947) ·201

America is the only nation in history which miraculously has gone directly from barbarism to degeneration without the usual interval of civilisation.

Georges Clemenceau ·200

Their demeanor… is invariably morose, sullen, clownish, and repulsive. I should think there is not, on the face of the earth, a people so entirely distitute of humour, vivacity, or the capacity of enjoyment.

Charles Dickens is decidedly unimpressed by the American people ·202

The only real native of Kansas is the buffalo. He's got a very hard head, a very uncertain temper, and a very lonely future. Apart from that, there's hardly any comparison between you.

Errol Flynn as Wade Hatton to Olivia De Havilland in *Dodge City* ·203

A big hard-boiled city with no more personality than a paper cup.

Raymond Chandler on LA, *The Little Sister*, 1949.·204

New York makes one think of the collapse of civilisation, about Sodom and Gomorrah, the end of the world. The end wouldn't come as a surprise here. Many people already bank on it. Saul Bellow,
Mr Sammler's Planet
(1970) ·205

How DOES America live with itself? Just by FORGETTING itself? Like an incontinent old man: stinks but ain't sure WHY. American novelist
Lucy Ellmann ·206

In Australia,
Inter alia,
Mediocrities
Think they're Socrates.

Peter Porter, unpublished clerihew; in
Stephen Murray-Smith (ed.), *The Dictionary
of Australian Quotations* (1984) ·207

And what has China
ever given the world?
Can you really respect
a nation that's never
taken to cutlery?

Victoria Wood ·208

Afrikaans sounds like
Welsh with attitude
and emphysema.

A.A. Gill ·209

To speak with your mouth full
And swallow with greed
Are national traits
Of the travelling Swede.

Duff Cooper; in Philip Ziegler,
Diana Cooper (1981) ·210

The best that can be said for Norweigan television is that it gives you the sensation of a coma without the worry and inconvenience.

Bill Bryson, *Neither Here Nor There* (1991) ·211

I don't like Norwegians at all. The sun never sets, the bar never opens, and the whole country smells of kippers.

Evelyn Waugh, *letter to Lady Diana Cooper,* 13 July 1934 ·212

In Italy for thirty years under the Borgias they had warfare, terror, murder, bloodshed — they produced Michelangelo, Leonardo da Vinci and the Renaissance. In Switzerland they had brotherly love, five hundred years of democracy and peace and what did they produce…? The cuckoo clock.

Orson Welles, *The Third Man* (1949 film); **Welles added these lines to Graham Greene's script** ·213

I look upon Switzerland as an inferior sort of Scotland. **Sydney Smith, *letter to Lord Holland,*** 1815 ·214

Frogs… are slightly better than Huns or Wops, but abroad is unutterably bloody and foreigners are fiends.

A little bit of xenophobia from Nancy Mitford, *The Pursuit of Love* (1945) ·215

Let's be frank, the Italians' technological contribution to humankind stopped with the pizza oven.

Bill Bryson, *Neither Here Nor There* (1991) •216

Every wise and thoroughly worldy wench

Knows there's always something fishy about the French!

Noël Coward, *'There's Always Something Fishy About the French'* •217

I hate the French, I hate them all From Toulouse Lafucking Trec to Charles de Gaulle.

Paul Scott Goodman, *'I Hate the French'* (from the musical *Bright Lights, Big City,* 1988, after the book by Jay McInerney) •218

He took offence at my description of Edinburgh as the Reykjavik of the South.

Tom Stoppard, *Jumpers* (1972) ·219

The land of my fathers. My fathers can have it.

Dylan Thomas of his Welsh homeland, *Adam* December 1953 ·221

It requires a surgical operation to get a joke well into a Scotch understanding.

Sidney Smith ·220

The English are, I think the most obtuse and barbarous people in the world.

Stendhal (Marie Henri Beyle) ·222

I've noticed that the English are not given to it.

Gore Vidal, on the suggestion that, in his books, washing has some symbolic significance; attrib., in *The Guardian* February 1999 ·224

For 'tis a low, newspaper, humdrum, lawsuit, Country.

Lord Byron, of England, *Don Juan* (1819-24) ·223

An Englishman thinks he is moral when he is only uncomfortable.

George Bernard Shaw, *Man and Superman* (1903) ·225

There is nothing good to be had in the country, or if there is, they will not let you have it.

William Hazlitt, *The Round Table* (1817) ·226

One has no great hopes for Birmingham. I always say there is something direful in the sound.

Mrs Elton in Jane Austen's *Emma* (1816) ·227

*Come,
friendly
bombs,
and
fall
on
Slough!
It
isn't
fit
for
humans
now.*

John Betjeman, *'Slough'* (1937) **·228**

I would like to live in Manchester, England. The transition between Manchester and death would be unnoticeable.

Mark Twain ·229

Immigrant, n.
An unenlightened
person who thinks
one country better
than another.

Ambrose Bierce, *The Devil's Dictionary*
(1911) ·230

PARTY PIECES

…when political ammunition runs low,
inevitably the rusty artillery of abuse
is always wheeled into action.

Adlai Stevenson, speech, 1952 ·231

He was a man of splendid abilities but utterly corrupt. Like rotten mackerel by moonlight, he shines and stinks.

John Randolph (1773-1833), member of the House of Representatives for Roanoak, Virginia, on jurist and statesman Edward Livingstone. ·232

Alexander Smith: You, sir, speak for the present generation, but I speak for posterity. Henry Clay: Yes, and you seem resolved to speak until the arrival of your audience.

Henry Clay, in the U.S. Senate; Robert V. Remini, *Henry Clay* (1991) ·233

John Randolph: I never sidestep skunks. Henry Clay: I always do.

American politician Henry Clay unexpectedly moved out of the way of his political rival John Randolph of Roanoke; in Robert V. Remini, *Henry Clay* (1991) ·234

He has all the characteristics of a dog except loyalty.

Texan hero Sam 'The Raven' Houston on fellow soldier and legislator Thomas Jefferson Green ·235

s

Even wisdom from him seems but folly.

The New York Post take an unsympathetic view of Abraham Lincoln. ·236

…We did not conceive it possible that even Mr Lincoln would produce a paper so slipshod, so loose-joined, so puerile, not alone in literary construction but in its ideas, its sentiments, its grasp. He has outdone himself. He has literally come out of the little end of his own horn. By the side of it, mediocrity is superb.

A contemporary review of Lincoln's Gettysburg Address from the *Chicago Times,* 1863. ·237

They never open their mouths without subtracting from the sum of human knowledge.

Thomas Reed (1839-1902), **Speaker of the US House of Representatives, on members of Congress** ·238

Heckler: I'm a Democrat! Theodore

Roosevelt: May I ask the gentleman why he is a Democrat?

Heckler: My grandfather was a Democrat; my father was a Democrat; and I am a Democrat.

Roosevelt: My friend, suppose your grandfather had been a jackass and your father was a jackass, what would you be?

Heckler (without hesitation): A Republican!

Theodore Roosevelt grapples with a heckler and loses ·239

He has no more backbone than a chocolate éclair.

Theodore Roosevelt on William E. McKinley ·240

My father always wanted to be the corpse at every funeral, the bride at every wedding and the baby at every christening.

Alice Roosevelt Longworth, on President Theodore Roosevelt, quoted in *Celebrity Register*, 1963 ·241

One always thinks of him as a glorified bouncer engaged eternally in cleaning out barrooms — and not too proud to gouge when the inspiration came to him, or to bite in the clinches.

H.L. Mencken on Theodore Roosevelt, *Prejudices, Second Series,* (1920) ·242

He writes the worst English that I have ever encountered. It reminds me of a string of wet sponges; it reminds me of tattered washing on the line; it reminds me of stale bean soup, of college yells, or dogs barking idiotically through endless nights.

H.L. Mencken, on US President Warren G. Harding, *Baltimore Evening Sun,* 1921 •243

His speeches left the impression of an army of pompous phrases moving over the landscape in search of an idea.

William G. McAdoo, Democratic, on Warren G. Harding •244

He looks as if he had been weaned on a pickle.

Alice Roosevelt Longworth, on Calvin Coolidge. ·245

Suffering from halitosis of the intellect. That's presuming Emperor Long has an intellect.

Secretary of the Interior Harold L. Ickes (1874-1952), **on Senator Huey Long** ·246

Never underestimate a man who overestimates himself.

Franklin D. Roosevelt, on General Douglas MacArthur ·247

One third Eleanor and two-thirds mush.

Alice Roosevelt Longworth (daughter of President Teddy), on Franklin D. Roosevelt ·248

My choice early in life was either to be a piano-player in a whorehouse or a politician. And to tell the truth, there's hardly any difference.

Harry S. Truman, 1962 ·249

A triumph for democracy. It proves that a millionaire has just as good a chance as anybody else.

Bob Hope, on John F. Kennedy's electoral victory in Wisconsin; on a 1960 TV programme, recalled in William Robert Faith, *Bob Hope* (1983) ·250

Not unlike Hitler, but without the charm.

Gore Vidal on conservative journalist Willam F. Buckley Jr, who he'd dubbed a 'crypto-Nazi' during a televised debate in 1968 ·252

Reading a speech with his usual sense of discovery.

Gore Vidal, of former-President Eisenhower at the Republican convention of 1964 ·251

Now listen, you queer, stop calling me a crypto-Nazi or I'll sock you in your goddamn face, and you'll stay plastered

Buckley's response to the crypto-Nazi comment. ·253

He is the kind of politician who would cut down a redwood tree and then mount the stump to make a speech for conservation.

Adlai Stevenson on Nixon ·254

I may not know much, but I know chicken shit from a chicken salad.

Lyndon Baines Johnson, on a speech by Richard Nixon; Merle Miller, *Lyndon* (1980) ·255

He can lie out of both sides of his mouth at the same time, and if he ever caught himself telling the truth, he'd lie just to keep his hand in.

Harry Truman on Richard Nixon ·256

Nixon's motto, if two wrongs don't make a right, try three.

Laurence J. Peter ·257

A group of politicians deciding to dump a President because his morals are bad is like the Mafia getting together to bump off the Godfather for not going to church on Sunday.

Russell Baker on Nixon and the Watergate scandal, *The New York Times,* 1974. ·258

Richard Nixon impeached himself. He gave us Gerald Ford as his revenge.

Bella Abzug in *Rolling Stone;* in Linda Botts, *Loose Talk* (1980) ·259

He looks like the guy in a science fiction movie who is the first to see the Creature.

David Frye on Gerald Ford ·260

So dumb he can't fart and chew gum at the same time.

Lyndon Baines Johnson, of Gerald Ford, in Richard Reeves, *A Ford, not a Lincoln* (1975) ·261

A triumph of the embalmer's art.

Gore Vidal, of Ronald Reagan; in *Observer*, 26 April 1981 ·262

I believe that Ronald Reagan can make this country what it once was — an Arctic region covered with ice.

Steve Martin ·263

The battle for the mind of Ronald Reagan was like the trench warfare of World War I. Never have so many fought so hard for such barren terrain.

Peggy Noonan; *What I Saw at the Revolution* (1990) ·265

A senescent bimbo with a lust for home furnishings

Barbara Ehrenreich on Nancy Reagan ·266

People here may be sharply divided over the Reagan administration's politics — but they admire Ronald Reagan for not getting involved in them.

Edward Kennedy Democratic Senator ·264

Washington couldn't tell a lie, Nixon couldn't tell the truth and Reagan couldn't tell the difference.

Mort Sahl, American comedian. ·267

Poor George, he can't help it — he was born with a silver foot in his mouth.

Former Texas governor Ann Richards, of George Bush Snr., in a keynote speech at the Democratic convention; in *Independent*, July 1988 ·268

An empty suit that goes to funerals and plays golf.

Ross Perot on Vice President Dan Quayle ·269

1. Not-Nearly-Curious-Enough George
2. The Americanian (after Bush referred to Greeks as 'Greecians' and Kosovars as 'Kosovarians')
3. The Global Village Idiot.

A selection of nicknames for 'Dubya' from *toostupidtobepresident.com*'s list of the *'Top 11 things international leaders already call George W. Bush behind his back'* ·270

Political pundits are saying President George W. Bush has made gains in two key states: dazed and confused

David Letterman ·271

Both candidates now are trying to lower expectations for how they'll do on the debates. For example, Kerry tried to lower expectations for himself by saying Bush has never lost a debate and that he is a formidable opponent. Then Bush lowered expectations for himself when he said, 'Hey, what does formidable mean?

Jay Leno, on the televised debates between Bush and Sen. John Kerry in the run-up to the 2004 presidential election. ·272

The president finally explained why he sat in that classroom on 9/11 for 7 minutes after he was told the country was under attack. He said he was 'collecting his thoughts.' What a time to start a new hobby.

Bill Maher ·273

He is probably choking on a pretzel or something. I hope nobody tells him that I have won this award while he is eating a pretzel… He has the funniest lines in the film. I am eternally grateful to him.

Michael Moore on President Bush, after winning the *Palme d'Or* award at the Cannes film festival for his documentary *Farenheit 9/11* ·274

I would like to apologize for referring to George W. Bush as a 'deserter.' What I meant to say is that George W. Bush is a deserter, an election thief, a drunk driver, a WMD liar, and a functional illiterate. And he poops his pants.

Michael Moore •275

No one ever went broke underestimating the taste of the great American public.

H.L. Mencken •276

If I knew them, it might spoil the purity of my hatred.

Norman Shrapnel explains his avoidance of MPs to fellow columnist Simon Hoggart; in *Guardian,* 3 February 2004 ·277

If it's a boy, I'll call it after myself. If it's a girl, I'll call it Victoria, after our Queen. But if, as I strongly suspect, it's nothing but piss and wind, I'll call it after you.

Australian PM Sir George Reid, on being asked by journalists what he was going to christen his corpulent stomach ·278

This little flower, this delicate little beauty, this cream puff, is supposed to be beyond personal criticism… He is simply a shiver looking for a spine to run up.

Paul Keating, of Australian Liberal leader John Hewson; in *Ned Sherrin in his Anecdotage* (1993); Harold Wilson is also said to have called Ted Heath 'a shiver looking for a spine to run up' ·279

Like being flogged with a warm lettuce.

Australian Prime Minister Paul Keating, referring to an attack by the opposition leader, John Hewson ·280

For socialists, going to bed with the Liberals is like having oral sex with a shark.

Larry Zolf comments on the Canadian political scene, 1975. ·281

On having encountered a voter who declared that he would sooner vote for the devil than vote for Wilkes: And your friend is not standing?

English radical and parliamentary reformer John Wilkes (1727-97); in Raymond Postgate, *'That Devil Wilkes'* (1956 rev. ed.) ·283

Boswell: So, Sir, you laugh at schemes of political improvement. Johnson: Why, Sir, most schemes of political improvement are very laughable things.

Samuel Johnson; in James Boswell, *Life of Samuel Johnson* (1791) **26 October 1769** ·282

Earl of Sandwich: *'Pon my soul, Wilkes, I don't know whether you'll die upon the gallows or of the pox.*
Wilkes: *That depends, my Lord, on whether I embrace your Lordship's principles, or your Lordship's mistress.*

John Wilkes; in Sir Charles Petrie, *The Four Georges* (1935); probably apocrypal ·284

Richard Brinsley Sheridan's son Tom declared that when he became an MP, he would proclaim his independence of party by emblazoning his forehead with the words 'To Let'. His father replied: 'And, under that, Tom, write 'unfurnished'.

Richard Brinsley Sheridan; Walter Jerrold, *Bon-Mots* (1893) ·285

The Right Honourable Gentleman is indebted to his memory for his jests and to his imagination for his facts.

Playwright and MP Richard Brinsley Sheridan (1751-1816), on the Earl of Dundad ·286

He is a self-made man, and worships his creator.

Conservative MP Benjamin Disraeli on Liberal statesman and radical Corn Law activist John Bright. ·287

The Right Honourable Gentleman is reminiscent of a poker. The only difference is that a poker gives off occasional signs of warmth.

British Conservative politician Benjamin Disraeli (1804-1881), **of former Conservative Prime Minister Sir Robert Peel** ·288

The ministers [on the Treasury Bench] reminded me of one of those marine landscapes not very uncommon on the coast of South America. You behold a range of exhausted volcanoes. Not a flame flickers on a single pallid crest.

Benjamin Disraeli, speech at Manchester, April 1872 ·289

He has not a single redeeming defect.

Benjamin Disraeli on W.E. Gladstone ·290

He made his conscience not his guide but his accomplice.

Benjamin Disraeli on W.E. Gladstone ·291

A sophisticated rhetorician, inebriated with the exhuberance of his own verbosity.

Benjamin Disraeli parodies Gladstone's high-falutin' style; in *The Times*, July 1878 ·292

On being asked to distinguish between a misfortune and a calamity:

If Gladstone fell into the Thames, that would be a misfortune, and if anybody pulled him out that, I suppose, would be a calamity.

Benjamin Disraeli ·293

His impact on history would be no more than the whiff of scent on a lady's purse.

David Lloyd George, on Arthur Balfour, British PM 1902-1905 ·294

He might make an adequate Lord Mayor of Birmingham in a lean year.

David Lloyd George on Neville Chamberlain; in Leon Harris, *The Fine Art of Political Wit* (1965) ·295

A very weak-minded fellow I am afraid, and, like the feather pillow, bears the marks of the last person who has sat on him!

British army commander Earl Haig describes the 17th Earl of Derby; in a *letter to Lady Haig,* 1918. (Often mistakenly attrib. to Lloyd George.) ·296

He was brilliant to the top of his army boots.

David Lloyd George on General Haig ·297

My vigour, vitality and cheek repel me. I am the kind of woman I would run away from.

Nancy Astor, British politician. ·298

The worst thing I can say about democracy is that it has tolerated the Right Honourable Gentleman [Neville Chamberlain] for four and a half years.

Aneurin ('Nye') Bevan, speech in the House of Commons 23 July 1929 ·299

Listening to a speech by Chamberlain is like paying a visit to Woolworth's: everything in its place and nothing above sixpence.

British Labour politician Aneurin Bevan (1897-1960), on Conservative MP and Prime Minister Neville Chamberlain. ·300

The Right Honourable and Learned Gentleman has twice crossed the floor of this House, each time leaving behind a trail of slime.

David Lloyd George on Sir John Simon ·301

His fame endures; we shall not forget The name of Baldwin until we're out of debt.

Kensal Green on Conservative politician and Prime Minister Stanley Baldwin (PM 1923-4 1924-9, 1935-7). ·302

Of course I believe in the Devil. How else would I account for the existence of Lord Beaverbrook?

Evelyn Waugh, of British newspaper proprietor and Conservative politician Max Aitken,1st Baron Beaverbrook; in L. Gourlay, *The Beaverbrook I Knew* (1984) ·303

I remember, when I was a child, being taken to the celebrated Barnum's circus, which contained an exhibition of freaks and monstrosities; but the exhibit on the programme which I most desired to see was the one described as 'The Boneless Wonder'. My parents judged that the spectacle would be too revolting and demoralizing for my youthful eyes, and I have waited fifty years to see 'The Boneless Wonder' sitting on the Treasury Bench.

Winston Churchill, of Labour politician Ramsay MacDonald; speech recorded in *Hansard*, 28 January 1931 ·304

[Churchill] would make a drum out of the skin of his mother in order to sound his own praises.

David Lloyd George; in Paul Johnson (ed.), ***The Oxford Book of Political Anecdotes*** **(1986); a similar comment about Churchill is attributed to Margot Asquith ·305**

Bessie Braddock, MP:

  Winston, you're drunk!
Churchill:

  Bessie, you're ugly. But tomorrow I shall be sober.

A legendary exchange between Bessie Braddock and Churchill. ·306

Mr Gladstone read Homer for fun, which I thought served him right.

Churchill ·307

If you wanted nothing done, Arthur Balfour was the best man for the task. There was no equal to him.

Churchill on Arthur Balfour (Conservative politician, and Prime Minister 1902-6) ·308

In the depths of that dusty soul there is nothing but abject surrender.

Churchill on Chamberlain ·309

We know that he has, more than any other man, the gift of compressing the largest amount of words into smallest amount of thought.

Winston Churchill on Ramsay Macdonald, 1933 ·310

Who is this man whose name is neither one thing nor the other?

Winston Churchill, of MP and prominent architect Alfred Bossom; attrib. ·311

He occassionally stumbled over the truth, but hastily picked himself up and hurried on as if nothing had happened.

Winston Churchill, of British Conservative politician Stanley Baldwin; in J.L. Lane (ed.), *The Sayings of Winston Churchill* (1992) ·312

The only recorded instance in history of a rat swimming towards a sinking ship.

Winston Churchill, of a former Conservative who proposed to defect to the Liberals; Leon Harris, *The Fine Art of Political Wit* (1965) ·313

What can you do with a man who looks like a female llama surprised when bathing?

Winston Churchill on Charles de Gaulle; in conversation, c.1944; David Fraser Alanbrooke *(1982)* ·314

I sympathize with General von Thoma. Defeated, humiliated, in captivity, and… (long pause for dramatic effect)… dinner with Montgomery.

Churchill, after Monty controversially invited a captive German General to dine with him. ·315

In defeat, unbeatable; in victory, unbearable.

Churchill on Montgomery ·316

[Clement Atlee] is a modest man who has a great deal to be modest about.

Winston Churchill on Clement Atlee, Labour politician and his successor as Prime Minister in 1945; in *Chicago Sunday Tribune Magazine of Books* June 1954 ·317

A sheep in sheep's clothing.

Winston Churchill on Clement Atlee; in Lord Home, *The Way the Wind Blows* (1976) ·318

They are not fit to manage a whelk stall.

Churchill on the Labour Party in 1945 ·319

He has all the virtues I dislike and none of the vices I admire.

Churchill on Stafford Cripps ·320

A merchant of discourtesy.

Churchill on Nye Bevan ·321

I welcome this opportunity of pricking the bloated bladder of lies with the poniard of truth.

Aneurin Bevan on Winston Churchill ·322

If you recognize anyone, it does not mean that you like him. We all, for instance, recognize the honourable Member of the Ebbw Vale.

Churchill uses Britian's recognition of Communist China to have a pop at his old adversary, Nye Bevan ·323

He is a man suffering from petrified adolescence.

Nye Bevan on Churchill ·324

*Lady Astor: If I were your wife I would put poison in your coffee!
Churchill: And if I were your husband I would drink it.* **A legendary exchange between Churchill and Lady Astor; in Consuelo Vanderbilt Balsan, *Glitter and Gold* (1952)** ·325

I am not going to spend any time whatsoever in attacking the foreign secretary. Quite honestly I am beginning to feel quite sorry for him. If we complain about the truth, there is no reason to attack the monkey when the organ grinder is present.

Aneurin Bevan, preferring to enter into debate with PM Churchill than Foreign Secretary Eden ·326

Lord Birkenhead is very clever but sometimes his brains go to his head.

Margot Asquith on Conservative politician and lawyer F.E. Smith, 1st Earl of Birkenhead; in *Listener* 11 June 1953, *'Margot Oxford' by Lady Violet Bonham Carter* ·327

An overripe banana, yellow outside, squishy in.

Sir Reginald Paget on Anthony Eden ·328

He enjoys prophesying the imminent fall of the capitalist system and is prepared to play a part, any part, in its burial — except that of a mute.

Conservative politician and Prime Minister Harold Macmillan, on the perpetually vocal Nye Bevan ·329

That's the trouble with Anthony — half mad baronet, half beautiful woman.

R.A. Butler, of British Conservative politician and Prime Minister Anthony Eden; attrib. ·330

He was not only a bore; he bored for England.

Malcolm Muggeridge of Anthony Eden; *Tread Softly* (1966) ·331

If Harold Wilson ever went to school without any boots, it was merley because he was too big for them.

Harold Macmillan casts aspersions on Harold Wilson's claims of a poor upbringing ·332

Dull Alec versus Smart Alec.

David Frost compares Alec Douglas-Home and Harold Wilson; in *That Was The Week That Was,* 1963 ·333

Randolph Churchill went into hospital… to have a lung removed. It was announced that the trouble was not 'malignant'… It was a typical triumph of modern science to find the only part of Randolph that was not malignant and remove it.

Evelyn Waugh on Winston's son; *'Irregular Notes 1960-65'; diary* March 1964 ·334

I do not often attack the Labour Party. They do it so well themselves.

Edward Heath, speech, 1973. ·335

Tory MP John Blackburn:
Mr Speaker, I am very
disappointed in you.
**George Thomas, Speaker
of the House of Commons:**
Why is that, John?
Blackburn: Well, Mr Speaker,
you have denied the House the
opportunity to hear a brilliant
speech on this subject. I have in
my pocket here a splendid speech
and by not calling me you have
denied the House the opportunity
to hear this, the best speech I have
ever prepared.
Thomas: It's always the same with
you, John, isn't it?
Blackburn: What do you mean,
Mr Speaker?
Thomas: Whenever I don't call you,
you have prepared the most brilliant
speech of all time, yet whenever
I do call you, you deliver a
fucking awful one.

Parliamentary exchange,
as told by Blackburn himself. ·336

*He represents what
I despise the most —
sanctimony, guile, slime
and intrigue under a
cloak of decency, all
for self-advancement
— it's called hypocrisy.*

Presumably the subject, Willie Whitelaw,
had offended Nicholas Fairbairn ·337

*The Labour Party is going
around stirring up apathy.*

William Whitelaw; recalled by Alan Watkins
as a characteristic 'Willieism'; in *Observer*,
May 1983 ·338

Child: *Mamma, are Tories born wicked, or do they grow wicked afterwards?* **Mother**: *They are born wicked, and grow worse.*

Anonymous, in G.W.E. Russell, *Collections and Recollections* (1898) ·339

The reason that there are so few female politicians is that it is too much trouble to put make-up on two faces.

Maureen Murphy ·340

Attila the Hen.

Clement Freud on Margaret Thatcher ·341

She sounded like the Book of Revelations read out over a railway station public address system by a headmistress of a certain age wearing calico knickers.

Clive James of Margaret Thatcher (on television, quoted in *Observer,* 1979) ·342

I cannot bring myself to vote for a woman who has been voice-trained to speak to me as though my dog had just died.

Keith Waterhouse, English humorist, on Margaret Thatcher ·343

Margaret Thatcher says she has given the French President a piece of her mind — this is not a gift I would receive with alacrity.

Denis Healey ·344

She is a half-mad old bag-lady. The Finchley whinger.

Tony Banks on Thatcher ·345

She is about as environmentally friendly as the bubonic plague.

Tony Banks on Thatcher ·346

She is a petty-minded xenophobe who struts around the world interfering and lecturing in an arrogant and high-handed manner.

Tony Banks on Thatcher ·347

[Margaret Thatcher] surprised everyone by buying a house in Dulwich instead of moving to Bolivia with the rest of the Nazis.

Jo Brand ·348

A Prime Minister whose self-righteous stubbornness has not been equalled, save briefly by Neville Chamberlain, since Lord North.

Roy Jenkins, of Margaret Thatcher, in *Observer* March 1990 ·349

I still think she should be strung up by the bollocks.

Jo Brand on Margaret Thatcher ·350

Rejoice, rejoice, rejoice.

Telephone call to Edward Heath's office following Margaret Thatcher's fall from power in 1990; attrib., in *Daily Telegraph* September 1998 *(online ed.)* ·351

Might as well have a corncob up his arse.

Alan Clark MP, on Douglas Hurd MP ·352

When he leaves the chamber, he probably goes to vandalise a few paintings somewhere. He is to the arts what Vlad the Impaler was to origami … He is undoubtedly living proof that a pig's bladder on a stick can be elected as a member of parliament.

Tony Banks on Tory MP Terry Dicks after the latter opposed state funding for the arts ·353

He is in government principally because of his ability to give a good news gloss to any disaster that turns up. He is a man who would have hailed the sinking of the Titanic as a first in underwater exploration. He would have greeted the Black Death as a necessary step towards a leaner and fitter economy. He would have celebrated the Great Fire of London as a vital contribution to urban regeneration.

Bryan Gould on David Mellor ·354

Neil Kinnock's speeches go on for so long because he has nothing to say, so he has no way of knowing when he's finished saying it.

John Major ·355

*He is so ambitious
that he squeaks
when he walks, and
cannot manage to
smile at any colleague
inferior in rank in
case he compromises
himself in some way.*

**Alan Clark, of Conservative Education Secretary
John Patten, in *Diaries — into Politics*, (2000)**
·356

*He has been described by John
Major as the minister for little
people — he seems more like
the minister for paperclips to me.*

**John Prescott on William Waldegrave's
appointment as the Secretary of State for
John Major's Citizens Charter ·357**

When I hear the name Richard Body I hear the sound of white coats flapping.

John Major, on one of his own MP's, 1994. attrib. ·358

At least it wasn't Ann Widdecombe.

Pat Dessoy, John Major's sister, on revelations about Major's 1980s affair with Edwina Currie. ·359

Is there no beginning to your talents?

Clive Anderson to Jeffrey Archer ·360

He has something of the night about him.

Tory MP Ann Widdicombe, on her former boss and Home Secretary Michael Howard, *1997* ·361

They used to be the Barmy Army. Now they're the Smarmy Army.

Michael Heseltine on the transformation of Labour into New Labour. ·362

If the church to which you went decided to stop worshipping God and started worshipping the devil, you would have second thoughts. the leadership of New Labour has abandoned their socialist faith and embraced capitalism which is tantamount to embracing the devil!

British trade union leader Arthur Scargill in *The Guardian*, May 1996 ·363

Peter Mandelson is a sweet guy, you know. But I eat lots of garlic and I sleep with garlic flowers round my neck. So I'm safe… for the moment.

Tony Banks on Peter Mandelson, May 1998 ·364

Peter Mandelson is someone who can skulk in broad daylight.

Simon Hoggart, in *The Guardian* July 1998 ·365

The effect is of a Womble taking Cerberus for a walk.

Will Cohn, of British Labour politician (and now life peer) Roy Hattersley and his dog Buster; in *Daily Telegraph* September 1998 ·366

My mum always told me to steer clear of redheads.

Frank Dobson on red-headed DJ Chris Evan's donation of £100,000 to Ken Livingstone's London mayor campaign ·367

I was very relieved when the child was born at the Chelsea and Westminster hospital. I had thought he would be born in a manger.

Leo Abse on the birth of Tony Blair's son Leo, in *Observer,* May 2000 ·368

Perhaps it is idealistic to suppose that any Minister might know their subject, but a passing interest is not beyond expectations.

Clare Balding, BBC sports presenter, on the lamentable performance of Richard Caborn, the new Minister for Sport, in her live sports quiz. ·369

John Prescott has the face of a man who clubs baby seals to death.

Denis Healey ·371

He was swaggering in a predatory way towards the susceptible of his conference like a gigolo eyeing the passenger deck.

Edward Pearce on Michael Portillo, in *The Guardian* ·370

Hell, I never vote for anybody. I always vote against.

W.C. Fields; in Robert Lewis Taylor,
W.C. Fields (1950) ·372

Here richly, with
  ridiculous display,
The Politician's corpse
  was laid away.
While all of his acquaintance
  sneered and slanged,
I wept: for I had longed
  to see him hanged.

British writer and Liberal politician
Hilaire Belloc (1870-1953) ·373

LIFE'S A BITCH

I'll bet your father spent the first year of your life throwing rocks at the stork.

Groucho Marx as J Cheever Loophole in *At The Circus* (1932) ·374

I married your mother because I wanted children. Imagine my disappointment when you arrived.

Groucho to Zeppo in
Horse Feathers ·375

I don't know what Scrope Davies meant by telling you I liked children, I abominate the sight of them so much that I have always had the greatest respect for the character of Herod.

Lord Byron, letter, 30 August 1811 ·376

The realization that it was not people I disliked but children was for me one of those celebrated moments of revelation.

Philip Larkin on his adolescent epiphany;
in Required Writing (1983) ·377

Oh, for an hour of Herod!

Anthony Hope at the first night of
J.M. Barrie's play, Peter Pan; in
Dennis Mackail, The Story of JMB
(1941) ·378

If you ever become a mother, can I have one of the puppies?

Charles Pierce ·379

It's a pity it was not the parents, rather than her, who thought of birth control.

Muriel Spark, on Marie Stopes ·380

Isadora Duncan: You have the greatest brain in the world, and I have the most beautiful body; so we ought to produce the most perfect child.

George Bernard Shaw: What if the child inherits my body and your brain?

Shaw ·381

I am brought to bed of a son, who shall suck hatred to you with his milk, and that I intend to have a great many more, for the sole purpose of raising you up enemies. Marie de Sévigné ·382

If a man's character is to be abused, say what you will, there's nobody like a relation to do the business.
William Makepeace Thackeray, *Vanity Fair* (1847-8) ·383

Could you possibly whistle your father and put him back on his lead, please.
Alan Ayckbourn, *Sisterly Feelings* (1981) ·384

Isn't it a shame when cousins marry?

A familiar retort for silencing hecklers ·385

It is no use telling me there are bad aunts and good aunts. At the core, they are all alike. Sooner or later, out pops the cloven hoof.

P.G. Wodehouse, *The Code of the Woosters* (1938) ·386

Grannies are only cute on TV. In real life they're like Oxfam shops on legs. Pamela Stephenson ·387

'It wouldn't hurt us to be nice, would it?' 'That depends on your threshold of pain.'

George S. Kaufman isn't thrilled by the prospect of a visit from his aunt; in Howard Teichmann, *George S. Kaufman* (1973) ·388

But there, everything has its drawbacks, as the man said when his mother-in-law died, and they came down upon him for the funeral expenses.

Jerome K. Jerome, *Three Men in a Boat* (1889) ·389

Someone once said, Rumbold, that education is what is left when you have forgotten all that you have ever learned. You appear to be trying to circumvent the process by learning as little as possible.

Alan Bennett, *Forty Years On* (1969) ·390

I asked my teacher what an oxymoron was and he said, 'I don't know what an oxy is, bastard.'

Arthur Smith and Chris England, *An Evening with Gary Lineker* (1990) ·391

I went to a girls' school and it made me so stupid that I could barely remember how to breathe.

India Knight ·392

Stand firm in your refusal to remain conscious during algebra in real life, I assure you, there is no such thing as algebra. Frank Lebowitz ·393

Every man should have a college education in order to show him how little the thing is really worth.

American writer and editor Elbert Hubbard ·394

If a man is a fool, you don't train him out of being a fool by sending him to university. You merely turn him into a trained fool, ten times more dangerous.

Novelist Desmond Bagley ·395

Universities incline wits to sophistry and affectation.

Courtier and philosopher Francis Bacon, *Valerius Terminus of the Interpretation of Nature,* (1603) ·396

Very nice sort of place, Oxford, I should think, for people that like that sort of place. They teach you to be a gentleman there. In the Polytechnic they teach you to be an engineer or such like.

George Bernard Shaw, *Man and Superman* (1903) ·397

The average PhD thesis is nothing but the transference of bones from one graveyard to another.

American historian and folklorist J Frank Dobie, *A Texan in England* ·398

Like so many ageing college people, Pnin had long ceased to notice the existence of students on the campus.

Vladimir Nabokov, *Paris,* (1957) ·399

A graduation ceremony is an event where the commencement speaker tells thousands of students dressed in identical caps and gowns that individuality is the key to success.

American writer Cynthia Ozick, *'Women and Creativity.'* (1969) •402

What time he can spare from the adornment of his person he devotes to the neglect of his duties.

William Thompson on Jebb, his Greek tutor at Cambridge in the 19th century •400

Come forth, Lazarus! And he came fifth and lost the job.

James Joyce, *Ulysses* (1922) •403

No academic person is ever voted into the chair until he has reached the age when he has forgotten the meaning of the word 'irrelevant'.

Francis M. Cornford, *Microsmographia Academica* (1908) •401

Prisoner before Mr Justice Darling, objecting to being referred to as 'a professional crook': *I've only done two jobs, and each time I've been nabbed.*
Lord Darling: *It has never been suggested that you are successful in your profession.*

Lord Darling; in Edward Maltby, *Secrets of a Solicitor* (1929) •404

Silly old fool. I pushed him into a rose bush for that.

Anna Ford recalls when Sir Robin Day told her she got a job as newsreader only because men wanted to sleep with her ·405

A lawyer is a person who writes a ten-thousand-word document document and calls it a brief. **Franz Kafka** ·406

…all in all I'd rather have been a judge than a miner. And what is more, being a miner, as soon as you are too old and tired and sick and stupid to do the job properly, you have to go. Well, the very opposite applies with the judges.

Peter Cook, 'Sitting on a Bench', nightclub act, 1960s ·408

I confidently expect that we [civil servants] shall continue to be grouped with mothers-in-law and Wigan Pier as one of the recognized objects of ridicule.

Edward Bridges, Portrait of a Profession (1950) ·407

Philanthropist, n. A rich (and usually bald) old gentleman who has trained himself to grin while his conscience is picking his pocket.

Ambrose Bierce, *The Devil's Dictionary* (1911) •409

If at first you don't succeed, failure may be your style.

Quentin Crisp; in *Sunday Telegraph* September 1999 •410

You fiend — never before have I encountered such corrupt and foul-minded perversity. Have you ever considered a career in the Church?

Blackadder II, 'Money', 1986 •411

Let the Dean and Canons lay their heads together and the thing will be done.

Sydney Smith on a proposal to surround St. Paul's cathedral with a wooden pavement; in H. Pearson, *The Smith of Smiths* (1934) •412

To a clergyman who had thanked him for the enjoyment he'd given the world: And I thank you for all the enjoyment you've taken out of it.

Groucho Marx; in Joe Adamson, *Groucho, Harpo, Chico and sometimes Zeppo* (1973) •413

Religion?
The fashionable substitute for Belief.

Oscar Wilde, *The Picture of Dorian Gray*
(1891) •414

Born again? No, I'm not. Excuse me for getting it right the first time. Dennis Miller •415

We were skeptical Catholics. We believed Jesus walked on water. We just figured it was probably winter.

John Wing •416

If it turns out that there is a God, I don't think that he's evil. But the worst that you can say about him is that basically he's an underachiever.

Woody Allen, *Love and Death* (1975 film) •417

God, to whom, if he existed, I felt I should have nothing very polite to say.

John Mortimer, *Clinging to the Wreckage*
(1982) •418

Isn't God a shit?

Randolph Churchill finds God more awful than awe-inspiring while reading the *Bible* straight through for a bet; in Evelyn Waugh, *diary*,
11 November 1944 •419

Mr Salteena was an elderly man of 42.

Daisy Ashford, *The Young Visiters* (1919) ·420

The denunciation of the young is a necessary part of the hygiene of older people, and greatly assists the circulation of their blood.

Logan Pearsall Smith, *Afterthoughts* (1931) *'Age and Death'* ·421

Age is deformed, youth unkind,
We scorn their bodies, they our mind.

Thomas Bastard, *Chrestoleros* (1598) ·422

Here lies
Ezekial Aikle
Aged 102
The Good
Die Young

Epitaph found in East Dalhousie, Nova Scotia ·423

Only think of Mrs Holder's being dead! Poor woman, she has done the only thing in the world she could possibly do to make one cease to abuse her.

Jane Austen, *letter to her sister, Cassandra* ·424

He'd make a lovely corpse.

Charles Dickens, *Martin Chuzzlewit* (1844) ·425

Waldo is one of those people who would be enormously improved by death.

Saki, *Beasts and Superbeasts* (1914) ·426

God was very good to the world. He took her from us.

Bette Davis on Miriam Hopkins ·429

I hope I don't die before Harry Secombe. I don't want him singing at my funeral.

Spike Milligan jokes at memorial service for Alf Garnett creator Johnny Speight; also attrib. as a fax sent by Milligan to Secombe ·427

Well it only proves what they always say — give the public something they want to see, and they'll come out for it.

Red Skelton comments on the crowds attending the funeral of movie tycoon Harry Cohn, March 1958; **attrib. ·430**

What I like about Clive Is that he is no longer alive. There is a great deal to be said For being dead.

Edmund Clerihew Bentley, *'Clive'* (1905) ·428

*They say you shouldn't say
nothing about the dead unless
it's good. He's dead. Good.*

Jackie 'Moms' Mabley ·431

TOO MUCH TESTOSTERONE

I hate all sports as rabidly as a person who likes sports hates common sense.

H.L. Mencken ·432

*He wears a No. 10 jersey.
I thought it was his position
but it turns out to be his IQ.*

George Best on Paul Gascoigne ·433

*He's been very, very
lucky; an average
player who came
into the game
when it was short
of personalities.*

George Best on Kevin Keegan ·434

*He can't kick with his left
foot. He doesn't score many
goals. He can't head a ball.
And he can't tackle. Apart
from that he's all right.*

George Best's appraisal of David Beckham ·435

Becks hasn't changed since I've known him. He's always been a flash Cockney git.

Ryan Giggs' wry comment on
Becks' love of the limelight •436

I've just seen Gary Lineker shake hands with Jurgen Klinsmann — it's a wonder Klinsmann hasn't fallen over.

Ron Atkinson •437

He's the worst finisher since Devon Loch. When he's in a clear shooting position he's under orders to do just one thing… pass.

Atkinson on his own player,
Carlton Palmer •438

Carlton Palmer can trap the ball further than I can kick it.

And again •439

The ideal soccer board of directors should be made up of three men; two dead, and the other dying.

Tommy Docherty ·440

Tony Hateley had it all. The only thing he lacked was ability. **Docherty on Tony Hateley** ·441

He didn't look anything like a professional athlete when I first clapped eyes on him. In fact, there were times when he barely resembled a member of the human race.

Brian Clough on former Forest winger John Robertson ·442

It's just like playing alongside Barbara Streisand.

Mike Summerbee suggests Rodney Marsh isn't the best team player, 1973 ·443

Someone once said you could write down Barry's knowledge of management on a postage stamp. I would say you need to fold the stamp in half.

Steve Claridge on Barry Fry ·444

A complete and utter shit.

Barry Fry on former Barnet chairman, Stan Flashman ·445

You are talking about a man who spelt his name wrong on his transfer request.

Gary Megson on Jason Roberts ·446

Harry Redknapp lookalike requires cash for corrective surgery to avoid Bagpuss jibes.

***Private Eye* spoof ad** ·447

He looks like a pissed vampire.

Chris Donald, editor of *Viz*, on Alan Hansen ·448

They could put a parking meter next to Alan Hansen and I'd find it more interesting watching it click round.

Rodney Marsh is spot-on for once in his assessment of Peter Schmeichel's ability as a TV pundit ·449

If you've all got a passport clap your hands.

Terrace chant aimed at Fulham chairman, Mohamed Al-Fayed ·450

Golf is not a sport. Golf is men in ugly pants, walking.

Robin Williams ·451

I played like Doug Saunders and putted like Colonel Sanders.

Chi Chi Rodríguez ·452

It would be an act of unimaginable masochism to plough through a tape of Alliss commentary.

Marina Hyde on golf commentator Peter Alliss, in *The Guardian* ·453

My God, it looks like a wax museum!

George Low turns up at his first seniors event ·454

When Langer practices on his own, he can hold up a fourball.

Dave Musgrove, Bernhard's caddie ·455

***American tourist, having just sliced his tee shot out of bounds:** In our country, we call that a Mulligan. What you call it over here? **St Andrew's caddie:** A three.* ·456

Colin Montgomerie has a face like a warthog that has been stung by a wasp. **David Feherty** ·457

I keep thinking that I might go out and play like Jack Nicklaus, but instead it's more like Jacques Tati. **Feherty on himself** ·459

I don't know him but I've seen him smile and that's quite enough to put me off wanting to know anything about him. **Feherty on Phil Mickelson** ·458

Like an octopus falling out of a tree. **Feherty assesses Jim Furyk's swing** ·460

Top hats look 100% ridiculous on anybody, but on, for example, Willie Carson, it's like attaching a factory chimney to a bungalow.

Giles Smith, TV critic, on the Royal enclosure at Ascot ·461

Rowntree's ears are a stark warning of the aesthetic dangers of prolonged exposure to the rugby scrum... .they resemble those indeterminate, gristly things given to puppies to chew on.

Derek Potter, 2002, from *Down Among The Head Men* ·462

His shyness is derivative of not having a high intellect.

Scott Gibbs on Welsh rugby union colleague Gavin Henson ·463

The human equivalent of beige. **Linda Smith on Tim Henman** ·464

Journalist:
Have you and Stacey split up?
McEnroe:
I'd like you to quote that you guys are shit.

McEnroe shoots from the hip ·465

The little dictator with the Beatles haircut.

Paul Weaver (*The Guardian*) on Bernie Ecclestone ·466

A drunkard, a glutton and a hellraiser.

Ed Smith on Babe Ruth
Playing Hard Ball (2002) ·467

Gower: *Do you want Gatt a foot wider?*
Cowdrey (the bowler): *No, he'd burst.*

Chris Cowdrey's response to his captain's suggestion that Mike Gatting be moved in the slip cordon ·468

Bad luck, Sir — you were just getting settled in.

Yorkshire's Fred Trueman to a University batsman, clean bowled first ball after lengthy 'limbering-up' and gardening at the wicket ·469

Captain: *I want a fielder right under Hussain's nose.*
Ian Healy: *That could mean anywhere within three miles.*

Nasser Hussain told this one himself ·470

Mark Waugh: Fuck me, look who it is. Mate, what are you doing out here? There's no way you're good enough to play for England.
Jimmy Ormond: Maybe not, but at least I'm the best player in my family.
Ashes, 2001 •471

I don't like you, Reeve. I never have liked you. You get right up my nose, and if you come anywhere near me I'll rearrange yours.
David Lloyd •474

Shane Warne: I've been waiting for two years to have another bowl at you.
Daryl Cullinan: Looks like you spent most of it eating.
Reported by Simon Hughes in *Yakking Round The World* •472

Glenn McGrath: Why are you so fucking fat?
Eddo Brandes: Because every time I fuck your wife she gives me a biscuit.
Zimbabwean tail-ender Brandes fails to be intimidated by McGrath's abuse •475

So how's your wife, and my kids?
Rodney Marsh to Ian Botham •473

Greg Thomas (After beating the bat):
It's red, round and weighs about five ounces.

Viv Richards (after hammering
the next ball out of the ground):
You know what it looks like, now
go and fetch it. Viv shows why he's never an
ideal target for sledging ·476

A LOT OF YAKS

I am not the greatest conductor in this country. On the other hand, I am better than any damned foreigner.
Sir Thomas Beecham (1879-1961) •477

Why do we have to have all these third-rate foreign conductors around — when we have so many second-rate ones of our own?

Thomas Beecham; L. Ayre, *Wit of Music* (1966) ·478

Beethoven's last quartets were written by a deaf man and should only be listened to by a deaf man.

Sir Thomas Beecham on Ludwig van Beethoven ·479

I nearly trod in some once.

Sir Thomas Beecham, on Stockhausen ·480

I didn't know he'd been knighted. I knew he'd been doctored.

Thomas Beecham on fellow composer Malcolm Sargent's knighthood; attrib. ·481

What can you do with it? It's like a lot of yaks jumping about.

Thomas Beecham on the third movement of Beethoven's Seventh Symphony; in Harold Atkins and Archie Newman, *Beecham Stories* (1978) ·482

By God, no, if it had been I should have run away myself.

The Duke of Wellington, on being asked whether a performance of Beethoven's *The Battle of Vitoria* resembled the real battle ·483

Wagner has lovely moments but awful quarters of an hour.

Giacchino Rossini, said to Emile Naumann, April 1867 in E. Naumann, *Italienische Tondichter* (1883) ·484

The music of Wagner imposes mental tortures that only algebra has a right to inflict.

Paul de Saint-Victor on Richard Wagner

in *La Presse* ·486

Liszt's orchestral music is an insult to art. It is gaudy musical harlotry, savage and incoherent bellowings.

Boston Gazette on Franz Liszt ·487

I have been told that Wagner's music is better than it sounds.

Bill Nye, in *Mark Twain, Autobiography* (1924) ·485

I can compare Le Carnaval Romain by Berlioz to nothing but the caperings and gibberings of a big baboon, over-excited by a dose of alcoholic stimulus.

George Templeton Strong;
diary entry ·488

Very vile — a catarrhal or sternutatory concerto. One frequently recurring phrase is a graphic instrumentation of a fortissimo sneeze, and a long passage is evidently meant to suggest a protracted, agonised bravura on the pocket handkerchief.

George Templeton Strong on a concerto by Franz Liszt; *diary entry* ·489

The musical equivalent of blancmange.

Bernard Levin on Frederick Delius ·490

He is like a man who sits on a stove and then complains that his backside is burning.

Gilbert on Sullivan ·491

Another week's rehearsal with WSG & I should have gone raving mad. I had already ordered some straw for my hair.

Sullivan on Gilbert ·492

It's a pity the composer did not leave directions as to how flat he really did want it sung.

Review in *West Wilts Herald*, 1893; in Ned Sherrin, *Cutting Edge* (1984) ·493

I liked your opera. I think I'll set it to music.

Ludwing van Beethoven to a fellow composer ·494

People are wrong when they say the opera isn't what it used to be. It is what it used to be — that's what's wrong with it.

Noël Coward, *Design for Living* (1933) •495

David Alden, the director who has been responsible for some of the English National Opera's most ridiculously awful productions, was reported as saying:
"If the stage direction says 'she weeps', I like her to be laughing. That's the way my mind works. It's a favourite creative trick of mine."
Trick, yes, but creative it certainly isn't.

Charles Osborne in an article entitled *'Disaster Aria',* March 1996 •496

I allowed twenty-four hours to elapse before writing this review: if I had been forced to produce it immediately after leaving the opera house, my language would have been distressingly intemperate. To put it mildly, then, this was the worst production that I can remember having experienced of any opera, and the only completely unmoving one of Fidelio...

Throughout the evening, the stage looked an absolute mess, comically so when the grim reaper and the devil arrived in stilts in the final scene. The audience, which until then had behaved itself surprisingly well, finally hooted with glee when the devil's curtains managed to close around Pizarro only with a little help from Pizarro itself.

I do advise the hard-hearted to go and see this Fidelio: they'll have a good laugh.

Charles Osborne on Beethoven's opera *Fidelio* **at the Royal Opera House, London. In** *Jewish Chronicle,* July 1986 •497

What the Marx Brothers did to Verdi's 'Il trovatore' in 'A Night the Opera', ENO has now done to the same composer's 'A Masked Ball' at the London Coliseum… This production is set neither in the Sweden of Verdi's original nor the Boston for which he settled because of censorship restrictions — but in what looks like a derelict lunatic asylum whose former inmates are still loitering about.

Charles Osborne on a production of Verdi's *Un Ballo in Maschera* at the London Coliseum; in *Jewish Chronicle*, September 1989 •498

The third movement began with a dog howling at midnight, proceeded to imitate the repurgations of the less-refined lower-middle-class type of water-closet cistern, modulating thence into the mass snoring of a naval dormitory around dawn — and concluded inconsequentially with the cello reproducing the screech of an ungreased wheelbarrow.

Alan Dent on Bela Bartók •499

This version takes place not in ancient Peking,
but in the interior of a corrugated iron drum.
Its characters are dressed in a variety of styles,
randing over 1,000 years of fashion Some of them
creep around in slow motion, while the young Prince
of Persia, who is about to be executed, engages in
simulated homo-erotic sex with his executioner.
The courtiers Ping, Pang and Pong are portrayed as
figures out of American vaudeville… and a huge
banner in Act II informs us, unnecessarily and
inaccurately, that 3 Enigmas = Death. It gets worse.

**Charles Osborne on a production of Puccini's opera *Turandot*,
at the London Coliseum,** December 1995 ·500

> *Swans sing before they die:*
> *'twere no bad thing*
> *Should certain persons die*
> *before they sing.*

**Samuel Taylor Coleridge,
*'On a Volunteer Singer'*** (1834) ·501

Last year I gave several lectures on 'Intelligence and the Appreciation of Music Among Animals.' Today I am going to speak to you about 'Intelligence and Appreciation of Music Among Critics.' The subject is very similar.

Erik Satie (1866-1925); in Nat Shapiro (ed.)
An Encylopedia of Quotations about Music (1978) ·502

I have just read your lousy review buried in the back pages. You sound like a frustrated old man who never made a success, an eight-ulcer man on a four-ulcer job, and all four ulcers working. I have never met you, but if I do you'll need a new nose and plenty of beefsteak and perhaps a supported below.

Harry S. Truman to *Washington Post* music critic Paul Hume ·503

Jazz: Music invented for the torture of imbeciles.

Harry van Dyke ·504

I don't like country music — but don't mean to denigrate those who do. For those people who like country music, denigrate means to put down.

Bob Newhart ·505

She ought to be arrested for loitering in front of an orchestra.

Bette Midler on Helen Reddy ·506

Presley sounded like Jayne Mansfield looked — blowsy and loud and low.

Julie Burchill ·507

They are, in my mind, responsible for most of the degeneration that has happened, not only musically but also in the sense of youth orientation and politically, too. They are the people who made it first publicly acceptable to spit in the eye of authority.

Reverend Pat Robertson? No, Frank Sinatra on The Beatles ·508

Oh, I get it. You don't want to be cute any more.

Bob Dylan's reaction to *Sgt Pepper's* ·509

Does Ringo exist apart from his records?
Who cares? It's doubtful the cutesy-pie tracks
Richard Perry has turned into Ringo Records
will ever move a listener to do anything more
than reach for the radio dial and that's what's
so unnerving about these records. These cuts
— this 'No No Song', that thoughtless remake
of 'Only You', 'Oh My My', 'You're Sixteen' —
they're maddening only for their lack of personality,
depth, emotional commitment. They're so insubstantial
they're hardly fit objects to provoke boredom, much
less concern and despair. **Gene Sculatti, *Creem,*** March 1976 ·510

If I found her floating in my
pool, I'd punish my dog.

Joan Rivers on Yoko Ono ·511

This man has child-bearing lips. Joan Rivers on Mick Jagger ·512

He moves like a parody between a majorette girl and Fred Astaire.

Truman Capote on Mick Jagger ·513

At the Grammy Awards, Keith Richards became the first performer ever to accept a posthumous award in Britain.

Actually, I never liked Dylan's kind of music before, I always thought he sounded like Yogi Bear.

Mick Ronson ·515

I think that's just another word for a washed-up has-been.

Bob Dylan, on being an 'Icon' ·516

*Dylan to me is the perfect symbol of the anti-artist in our society. He is against everything —
the last resort of someone who doesn't really want to change the world... Dylan's songs accept the world as it is.*

Ewan MacColl on Bob Dylan,
Melody Maker, 1965 ·518

Watching this programme, there are moments when you'd swear that Bob Dylan was actually dead, in so emphatically past tense is the story told, so respectful, indeed quietly monumental is its tone. The voice-over could almost be reciting his obituary from The Times. And then, almost at the last minute in the final section which telescopes the last two decades into a fifth of the running time, the mood suddenly switches and we are reassured that Bob, far from being busy dyin', is busy being reborn (and not for the first time).

Mat Snow on Bob Dylan: ***The American Troubadour,*** for ***Rock's Backpages,***
March 2001 ·517

He plays four-and-a-half sets, That's torture. Does he hate his audience?

John Lydon about Bruce Springsteen ·519

He was so mean it hurt him to go to the bathroom.

Britt Ekland about Rod Stewart ·520

They didn't look like like humans. They looked like foetuses. I felt physically ill when I saw them on TV.

The ever-restrained Julie Burchill on Bay City Rollers ·521

He has Van Gogh's ear for music.

Orson Wells on 70's pop star Donny Osmond ·522

Five bowls of muesli looking for a spoon.

The New Musical Express on Yes ·523

If you looked up the word pretentious in the dictionary, you could possibly see a picture of Emerson, Lake and Palmer.

Carl Palmer •525

Like a foul alignment of all the black planets, this collection of 95-97 material culled from the Keys to Ascension I and II albums, saw all the important members of Yes […] reunited to wreak havoc on the world. Chords are played at random, tunes change tempo for no other reason than that is what happens in symphonies and tracks are long just for longness's sake… The fact that they had a hit single as recently as 15 years ago should serve as a warning to us all that this sort of thing could strike at any moment.

David Quantick reviews Yes's album
Keys to the Studio in *Q Magazine*,
September 2001 •524

In a cybernetic fit of rage
She pissed off to another age
She lives in 1999
With her new boyfriend,
a blob of slime.
Each time I see a
translucent face
I remember the monster
from outer space.

John Cooper Clarke, *I married a monster from outer space,* 1978 ·526

I'm not offended at all because
I know I'm not a dumb blonde.
I also know I'm not blonde.

Dolly Parton brushes her critics aside;
in M. Palmer, *Small Talk, Big Names:*
40 Years of Rock Quotes (1993) ·527

All legs and hair with a mouth
that could swallow the whole
stadium and the hot-dog stand.

Laura Lee Davies on Tina Turner ·528

You have to admire
her. She hides her lack
of talent so well.

Manola Blahnik, shoemaker, on Madonna ·529

*She's so hairy, when she lifted
her arm I thought it was
Tina Turner in her armpit.*

Joan Rivers on Madonna ·530

Bambi with testosterone.

Owen Gleiberman on Prince, in *Entertainment Weekly* ·531

*He looks like a dwarf who's been
dipped in a bucket of pubic hair.*

Boy George on Prince ·532

***Lovesexy*, it has to be said, is a turgid collection
of inconclusive riffs and weak melodies, decorated
to distraction by harsh and flashy ornamentation.**

**David Toop, on Prince's album *Love Sexy*,
in the *Sunday Times*, 22 May 1988** ·533

Michael Jackson's album was only called 'Bad' because there wasn't enough room on the sleeve for Pathetic.

Prince ·535

If you, like, make out with a frog, then you turn into Prince.

Butthead ·534

*After meeting Bono, it made me want to
give up being in a rock & roll band.*

Dave Grohl of Nirvana (1992) ·536

*The Celine Dion we know and love is a
handsome woman. That's not the way
I remember her from Eurovision.*

**Surely Mr Wogan isn't suggesting
a bit of nip and tuck?** ·537

It's hardly Paul McCartney leaving The Beatles.

Noel Gallagher, on Bonehead's departure from Oasis (1999) ·538

*I just wish Eddie Vedder
would get on with it and
kill himself.*

**Noel Gallagher of Oasis on
the Pearl Jam frontman,** 1996 ·539

She's got a face like a satellite dish and ankles like my granny's.

Robbie Williams on British pop star
Sophie Ellis Bextor ·540

And yes, making Posh Spice look dumb didn't turn out to be all that hard.

The Guardian columnist Zoe Williams ·541

We made it easy for them to come and nick things from us. They're sticky tape on a duck's arse.

The Sex Pistols' John Lydon questions
Green Day's originality ·542

The still-born brainchild of Korn bassist Reginald Fieldy Arvizu, Rock 'n' Roll Gangster is an utterly unlikeable gangsta-rap pastiche. When not tiresomely trumpeting his titanic weed intake, Fieldy stumbles through sterilised sex rhymes and banal B-boy bragging so devoid of charm or wit that they make the similarly salacious Kid Rock sound like Stephen Fry in comparison.

Dan Silver on the album *Rock 'n' Roll Gangster* by Fieldy's Dreams,
in *Q* magazine, January 2002 ·543

Three tracks in this truly lamentable opus and you'll have lost the will to live; four tracks and you'll be weeping openly into your coffee cup.

James Cooper on heavy metal band Solstice's album *Lamentations;* **in** *Kerrang,* August 2001 •545

In the 18-year old wake of David Bowie's 'Pin-Ups', few artists have been foolish enough to do a covers album. Duran Duran were the last notable culprits with 1995's inexplicable 'Thank You'; and now Simple Minds have decided to come after them… Really, to call this a turkey would be unfair to the birds who share the name.

John Harris on Simple Minds' *Neon Lights;* **in** *Q* **magazine,** October 2001 •544

Macho rap-rock from the UK. Horrible, horrible. This is the sound of five men in competition to prove who has the most testosterone.

Emma Johnston on nu-metal band Lillydamnwhite (album *Eviscerate*) in *Kerrang,* July 2001 ·546

This tragic bombardment of tuneless metal cliché fails to move in any direction other than towards the bin.

Steve Beebee on Debase's album *Domination,* in *Kerrang,* October 2001 ·547

Oh dear, oh dear. Second-rate teeny acts (Samantha Mumba, a1, S Club 7) or people who promised never to trouble us again (Lulu, Lisa Stansfield, Yazz, Erasure) sing Motown songs badly. And what on earth the admirable Chris Rea — neither second-rate nor teen fodder — is doing here is something he should be discussing with his advisors right now; as he sacks them. John Aizlewood on *Motown Mania,* by various artists, in *Q* magazine, March 2001 ·548

I did not watch the Brit awards on television last night. Recent experience suggests that such back-slap-athons are hazardous to my blood pressure. Indeed, simply reading about the Brits was quite enough to send me into a state of foaming apoplexy. Kylie, Dido, Travis, Westlife, S Club 7, Shaggy… and, topping it all off, Sting, emperor of wine-bar muzak. It was a line-up to make you howl, or at least despaire of pop ever meaning anything, well, meaningful again…

Chart pop has become so redundant, so musically bankrupt, that the best we can do is collude with the mass delusion that a pocket-sized Oz automaton is a spunky sex goddess with a flawless sense of irony. I refer, of course, to Ms Minogue, whose numbingly formulaic 'Can't Get You Out of My Head' is being hailed as some work of postmodern electro-pop genius… In the new global celebrity culture, pop literally means nothing other than fame.

Barney Hoskyns, Editorial Director of *Rock's Backpages*
in the *Independent*, 22 February 2002 ·549

TRASH(ING) TV

There you have it, Ladies and gentlemen: television — the next best thing to real entertainment. **David Letterman, quoted in** M Magazine, 1992 ·550

Television is an invention that permits you to be entertained in your living room by people you wouldn't have in your home.

David Frost ·551

At Hélène's party, during which her sensational norks are practically on the table among the sweetmeats, Pierre is asked to do a worried version of the bug-eyed act Sid James turns on when he is abruptly shoved up against Barbara Windsor.

Clive James on a BBC production of Tolstoy's *War and Peace,* 1972 ·552

On Talk-In (BBC1) Robin Day chaired a discussion of Miss World between a handful of Women's Libbers and the massed forces of darkness. Far from being the natural output of a male chauvinist pig, Day's arrogance goes beyond sex and indeed the bounds of credibility, to the point where you expected a flying wedge of ravening Maenads to spring from the audience and rip him to bits. Clive James in the *Observer,* December 1972 ·553

Wuthering Heights (BBC2) is the blithering pits.

Clive James in the *Observer,* October 1978 ·554

Towering Inferno had met The Poseidon Adventure. Actors who had spent their whole lives on the feature list held on to their hair transplants and shouted the line that had been haunting them in their sleep for years: We'll never make it!

Clive James on a mini-series, *Condominium: When the Hurricane Struck*, in the *Observer*, August 1981 •555

It occurs to me that it takes a rather special sort of person to follow soaps. You have to be highly intelligent (to understand them) and as thick as a brick (to want to). Alan Coren, *Mail On Sunday*, 1986. •556

UC: Undercover (10pm Sunday on NBC, Channel 3): Members of an elite Justice Department undercover squad get freaked out when they go undercover, wear head-to-toe black leather to blend in, and choke during the inevitable gunfights. Apparently, they don't understand the definition of elite.

Rick Kushman, in the *Sacramento Bee*, September 2001 •557

Her manner has been described as that of a dominatrix, but with her practical cropped hair and glasses, she is more like a school librarian in a black leather coat. Her insults are innocuous.

The New York Times on Anne Robinson's *The Weakest Link* •558

About as cuddly as a cornered ferret.

Lynn Barber on Anne Robinson, in *The Times* October 2001 •559

I'll put an ad in the papers. Wanted, kind home for enormous savage rodent. Answers to the name of Sybil.

Long-suffering' husband Basil Fawlty (John Cleese) looks to re-home his wife in *Fawlty Towers, 'Basil the Rat'* 1979 ·560

Hacker: Humphrey, do you see it as part of your job to help ministers make fools of themselves?
Sir Humphrey: Well, I never met one that needed any help

Paul Eddington and Nigel Hawthorne in *Yes, Minister, 'The Right to Know'* 1980 ·561

Ecological activist: There is nothing special about man, Mr. Hacker. We're not above nature. We're all part of it. Men are animals too, you know.
Hacker: I know that — I've just come from the House of Commons!
Yes, Minister, 'The Right to Know' 1980 ·562

A man like you needs something to reflect your image — I've got a lovely Skoda in the forecourt.

Boycie (John Challis) to Del Boy (David Jason), *Only Fools and Horses, 'He ain't heavy, he's my uncle',* BBC TV, 1991 ·563

Hey, girls, seen much of Cinderella since the wedding?

Del Boy encounters the 'Gruesome Twosome' sisters; *Only Fools and Horses* ·564

Sit down Rodney. Keep your brains warm. Derek 'Del Boy' Trotter to brother Rodney (Nicholas Lindhurst); *Only Fools and Horses* ·565

Boycie: I heard a rumour that Mickey Mouse wears a Rodney Trotter wristwatch.
Only Fools and Horses,'Video Nasty', ;1986 ·566

I am Holly, the ship's computer, with an I.Q. of 6000 — the same I.Q. as 6000 P.E. teachers.

Norman Lovett as Holly in *Red Dwarf*, *'Future Echoes'* 1988 ·567

Holly: *It's better to have loved and to have lost than to listen to an album by Olivia Newton-John.*
Cat: *Why's that?*
Holly: *Anything's better than listening to an album by Olivia Newton-John.*

Norman Lovett as Holly and Danny John-Jules as Cat in *Red Dwarf*, *'Stasis Leak'* 1988 ·568

Sam: *I've never met an intelligent woman I'd want to date.*
Diane: *On behalf of all the intelligent women in America, may I just say… whew!* Ted Danson and Shelley Long in *Cheers* ·569

Lilith: Well, I'm off. I don't know what the future holds. Whatever happens, I only hope I can realize my full potential. To acquire things the old Lilith never had.

Carla: Like a body temperature?

Lilith: That's very good, Carla. Incidentally, I've taken your little wisecracks for a few years now, you hideous gargoyle, and if you ever open that gateway to hell you call a mouth in my direction again, I'll snap off your extremities like dead branches and feed them to you at gunpoint.

Babe Neuwirth and Rhea Perlman in *Cheers* ·570

> *Frasier:* Oh, dad, she's not a weirdo. She's just a woman who finds me utterly fascinating.
> *Niles:* And the distinction would be?

Kelsey Grammer & David Hyde Pierce in *Frasier* ·571

> *Blackadder:* Baldrick! Thank you for introducing me to a genuinely new experience.
> *Baldrick:* What experience is that?
> *Blackadder:* Being pleased to see you. What are you doing here, you revolting animal?

Rowan Atkinson and Tony Robinson in *Blackadder the Third*, *'Amy and Amiability'*, 1987 BBC TV series ·572

Now, Bob, this is Percy: a smooth-shaving dimwit I don't seem to be able to shake off.

Rowan Atkinson introduces Percy (Tim McInnerny) to Bob (Gabrielle Glaister)
Blackadder II, 'Bells', 1986 ·573

Blackadder: Of course you know what your great discovery means, don't you, Percy?
Percy: Perhaps, my lord.
Blackadder: That you, Percy, Lord Percy, are an utter berk.

Blackadder is unimpressed by Percy's ability to turn base
metal into green. *Blackadder II,* 1986 ·574

*Well, now, look Dr Johnson, I may be as thick as a whale
omlette, but even I know that a book's got to have a plot.*

Hugh Laurie's Prince Regent is underwhelmed by Dr Johnson's dictionary;
Blackadder the Third, 'Ink and Incapability' 1987 ·575

Talbot: It minds me not that you dress like
  a mad parrot and talk like a plate of beans
  negotiating their way out of a cow's digestive system…

Prince George: *Good on you, sir.*

Talbot: It is no skin off my nose that there are
  bits of lemon peel floating down the Thames
  who would make better regents than you.

Prince George: *Well, bravo.*

Denis Lill and Hugh Laurie in *Blackadder the Third, 'Dish and Dishonety',* 1987 ·576

Blackadder: Look, mate, mate, me old mate… you've got nothing against me.
Ambassador: On the contrary, I hate you English. With your boring trousers and your shiny toilet paper and your ridiculous preconceptions that Frenchmen are great lovers. I'm French and I'm hung like a baby carrot and a couple of petit pois. **Chris Barrie as the Ambassador in *Blackadder the Third, 'Nob and Nobility'*,**1987 ·577

Mrs Miggins: You better watch out, Mr Blackadder. Things are bound to change.
Blackadder: Not while Pitt the Elder's Prime Minister. He's about as effective as a cat flap in an elephant house. And as long as his feet are warm and he gets a cup of nice milky tea in the sun before his morning nap, he doesn't bother anyone until his potty needs emptying.

***Blackadder the Third, 'Dish and Dishonety'*,**1987 ·578

Yes, it's not the only thing round here that's very small indeed. Your brain's so minute, Baldrick, that if a hungry cannibal cracked your head open, there wouldn't be enough to cover a small water biscuit.

Blackadder to Baldrick, in *Blackadder Goes Forth, 'Captain Cook'*, ·579

Yes. To you, Baldrick, the Renaissance was just something that happened to other people, wasn't it? **Blackadder II, 'Head', 1986** ·580

Baldrick, does it have to be this way?
Our valued friendship ending with me
cutting you up into strips and telling the
Prince that you walked over a very sharp
cattle grid in an extremely heavy hat?

Blackadder the Third, 'Duel and Duality', 1987 ·581

The most over-rated human being since Judas Iscariot
won the AD31 Best Disciple Competition.

Blackadder (of the Scarlet Pimpernel) in
Blackadder the Third, 'Nob & Nobility' ·582

Flashheart: *You must be pretty impressed, having Squadron*
Commander the Lord Flashheart drop in on your squalid bit of line!
Blackadder: *Actually, no — I was more impressed by the contents*
of my handkerchief the last time I blew my nose.

The arrival of Lord Flashheart (Rik Mayall) fails to cheer Blackadder
in Blackadder Goes Forth 'Private Plane' ·583

Baldrick, no! It's the worst plan since Abraham Lincoln said, 'Oh, I'm sick of kicking around
the house tonight, let's go take in a show.' For a start, General Melchett is in mourning for
the woman of his dreams — he's unlikely to be in the mood to marry a two-legged badger
wrapped in a curtain. Secondly, we are looking for a great entertainer and you're the worst
entertainer since St Paul the Evangelist toured Palestine with his trampoline act. No, we'll
have to find somebody else. **Blackadder's response to Baldrick's plan to marry General Melchett and**
become a leading lady, in Blackadder Goes Forth, 'Major Star' ·584

George, you were bloody awful... But you can't argue with the box office. Personally I thought you were the least convincing female impressionist since Tarzan went through Jane's handbag and ate her lipstick, but I'm clearly in a minority. Look out London. Here we come.

Blackadder to Hugh Laurie's George, after his show-stopping performance as the leading lady in an army gang show, in *Blackadder Goes Forth*, 'Major Star' ·585

Bravo, Blackadder! I have absolutely no hesitation appointing you our official regiment's artist. You're a damn good man — not a pen-pushing, desk-sucking, blotter-jotter like Darling, here, eh, Darling!

Stephen Fry as General Melchett in *Blackadder :Goes Forth, 'Captain Cook'* ·586

Melchett: *Well, that's that then — Blackadder.*
Blackadder: *Yes, sir?*
Melchett: *You are now Head of Operation Winkle.*
Blackadder: *Thank you, sir.*
Melchett: *Darling?*
Darling: *Yes, sir?*
Melchett: *You are a complete arse.*

Blackadder Goes Forth, 'General Hospital', ·587

Will you stand still when I'm talking to you! If by a man's works shall you know him, then you're a steaming pile of horse manure.

General Melchett to Blackadder in *Blackadder Goes Forth, 'Major Star'* ·588

My mother didn't give birth — she had something removed.

Joanna Lumley as Patsy in Jennifer Saunders'
Absolutely Fabulous, 'Iso Tank', 1992 ·589

Darling, if you want to talk bollocks and discover the meaning of life, you're better off downing a bottle of whiskey. At least that way, you're unconscious by the time you start to take yourself seriously. Patsy dispenses advice in *Absolutely Fabulous*, *'The End'*, 1995 ·590

One more facelift on this one and she'll have a beard.

Patsy again, in *Absolutely Fabulous, 'Iso Tank'* 1992 ·591

Damien Day: You were asking for it.
Dave Charnley: You putrid piece of rat droppings!
DD: Look, I told you, don't mess with the big boys.
DC: You dirty, conniving bastard!
DD: Look, I'm sorry, you're just not in my league.
DC: You have all the scruples of Mark Thatcher.
DD: Now look, careful, you can go too far.

The former-Prime Minister's son Mark is an
insult too far for Stephen Tompinkson (Damien)
and Neil Pearson (Dave) in *Drop the Dead Donkey* ·592

Caroline: I find men such enigmas. How do you find them, Sally?
Henry: She finds them in transport cafes, mostly.

David Swift as Henry in *Drop the Dead Donkey* ·593

Henry: I'm trying to fill in one of these National Lottery tickets.
I thought I'd put down the number of times I had sex last month,
but they don't go higher than 49.
Joy: Try sticking to the number of times someone else was there.

David Swift and Susannah Doyle in *Drop the Dead Donkey* ·594

Ted: Dougal, how did you get into
the church in the first place? Was it,
like, collect twelve crisp packets and
become a priest? Dermot Morgan as Father Ted Crilly in *Father Ted* ·595

Harmony: You love that tunnel more than me.
Spike: I love syphilis more than you.

Mercedes McNab (Harmony) and James Masters (Spike), in
Buffy the Vampire Slayer, 'The Harsh Light of Day' ·596

*She's the gnat in my ear. The gristle in my
teeth. The bloody thorn in my bloody side.*

James Masters as vampire Spike on 'sworn enemy' Buffy, in
Buffy the Vampire Slayer, 'What's My Line? Part 1' ·597

*Wesley: Remember the three key words for any slayer:
Preparation, Preparation, Preparation.*
Buffy: That's one word three times.

Wesley (Alexis Denisof) dispenses some advice to a sardonic Buffy in
Buffy the Vampire Slayer, 'Bad Girls' ·598

*It doesn't matter how you got here or where you
came from. You are my sister. There's no way you
could annoy me this much if you weren't.*

Buffy (Sarah Michelle Gellar) feels some sisterly love for Dawn
(Michelle Trachtenberg) , in *Buffy the Vampire Slayer, 'Blood Ties'* ·599

Devon: We gotta get a roadie. Other bands have roadies.
*Oz: Other bands know more than three chords. Your professional bands can
play up to six and sometimes seven completely different chords. Devon: That's
just like, fruity jazzy bands.* Jason Hall (Devon) and Seth Green
(Oz), in *Buffy the Vampire Slayer, 'Doppelgangland'* ·600

Cordelia: Willow! Hi. I like your outfit.
Willow: No, you don't.
Cordelia: No, I really don't. But I need a favour.

Charisma Carpenter (Cordelia) and Alyson Hannigan (Willow)
in *Buffy the Vampire Slayer, 'Prophecy Girl'* ·601

Buffy: We don't say 'Indian.'
Giles: Yes! Right. Always behind on the terms.
Still trying not to refer to you lot as 'bloody colonials.'

Buffy (Sarah Michelle Gellar) and Giles (Anthony Stewart Head) get all politically
correct in *Buffy the Vampire Slayer, 'Pangs'* ·602

*Well, there you go. Even when he's
good he's all Mr Billowy Coat of Pain.*

Marc Blucas's Riley gets a little jealous of Buffy's vampire ex, Angel, in
Buffy the Vampire Slayer, 'The Yoko Factor' ·603

Giles: I'm not supposed to have a private life?
Buffy: No, because you're very, very old, and it's gross.

Buffy the Vampire Slayer, 'The Freshman' ·604

Xander: We're part of the team. [Buffy] needs us.

Spike: Or you're just the same tenth-grade loser you've always been and she's too much of a softy to cut you loose.

Nicholas Brendon as Xander and James Masters as Spike in
Buffy the Vampire Slayer, 'Doomed' ·605

Cordelia: You were too busy rushing off to die for your beloved Buffy…You'd never die for me.

Xander: I might die from you, does that get me any points?

Buffy the Vampire Slayer, 'Innocence' ·606

I am Xander, King of the Cretins, and all lesser cretins must bow before me.

Buffy the Vampire Slayer, 'The Witch' ·607

I have a bad feeling that whenever a lesbian looks at me they think 'That's why I'm not a heterosexual'.

Jason Alexander as George in *Seinfeld* ·608

You are whiny. You are obsessive. You are insecure. You are gutless. You never just sort of seize the day. You liked me for what, a year and you didn't do anything about it, and uh, uh, you wear too much of that gel in your hair. Rachel to Ross, *Friends,*
'The One With Phoebe's Dad' ·609

Hell is filled with people like you.

Chandler to Monica, *Friends, 'The One With The Evil Orthodontist'* ·610

He proposed on a Valentine's day, although he didn't do it face to face, he did it in one of the little Valentine message bits in the paper. I think he had to pay for it by the word, because it just said 'Lee love Dawn, marriage?' which, you know I like, because it's not often you get something that's both romantic and thrifty. Lucy Davis as Dawn in *The Office*, Series 1 Episode 4 ·611

Gareth: In this room, I have special…
Tim (interrupting): Needs?
Gareth: No, I am a special…
Tim: Needs child?
Gareth: No. And that's not even funny.

Mackenzie Crook (Gareth) and Martin Freeman (Tim), in *The Office* S1E2 ·612

What was it that first attracted you to millionaire Paul Daniels?
Mrs Merton (Caroline Aherne) to Debbie McGhee *The Mrs Merton Show* ·613

You were a right old slapper in the seventies, weren't you?
Mrs Merton to Germaine Greer ·614

If you hadn't run around so much, maybe you wouldn't have been so thirsty.
Mrs Merton to George Best ·615

My show is the stupidest show on TV. If you're watching it, get a life.

Jerry Springer; in *Independent on Sunday*, March 1999 ·616

YOU'RE SO VAIN

Oh, the self-importance of fading stars. Never mind, they will all be black holes one day.

Jeffrey Bernard; in *The Spectator,* July 1992 •617

Lily wasn't exactly a beauty, though her eyes were; she just happened to be born in a day when standards were far lower and less exacting.

Rachel Ferguson on Lily Langtry •618

George: A Charlie Chaplin film! Oh, I love old Chappers, don't you, Cap?
Blackadder: Unfortunately, no I don't. I find his films about as funny as getting an arrow through the neck and then discovering there's a gas bill tied to it.

Hugh Laurie and Roawn Atkinson, *Blackadder Goes Forth'*, '*Major Star'*, (BBC TV, 1989) •619

Can't act. Slightly bald. Also dances.

A studio official comments on Fred Astaire; quoted by Bob Thomas *Astaire* (1985) •620

Katharine Hepburn: Thank goodness I don't have to act with you any more.
John Barrymore: I didn't know you ever had, darling.

The loving couple, after filming *A Bill of Divorcement* (1932) •621

She sounds more and more like Donald Duck.

Bette Davies on Katherine Hepburn •622

*I refuse to play golf with Errol Flynn.
If I want to play with a prick, I'll
play with my own.* W.C. Fields ·623

*That man's ears make him look like
a taxi-cab with both doors open.*

Howard Hughes Jr., of Clark Gable; in
Charles Higham and Joel Greenberg,
Celluloid Muse (1969) ·624

*Dietrich? That contraption! She was one
of the beautiful-but-dumb girls, like me,
but she belonged to the category of those
who thought they were smart and fooled
other people into believing it.*
Louise Brooks on Marlene Dietrich ·625

*Watching Spencer Tracy on the set of Dr Jekyll and Mr Hyde (1941):
Which is he playing now?* W. Somerset Maugham, attrib. In Leslie Halliwell,
The Filmgoer's Book of Quotes (1978 ed.) ·626

*Doris Day is as wholesome as a bowl
of cornflakes and at least as sexy.*

Dwight Macdonald, US critic ·627

When the bespangled Cyd Charisse wraps her phenomenal legs around Fred Astaire, she can be forgiven everything — even the fact that she reads her lines as if she learned them phonetically.

A sting in the tail from Pauline Kael in a review of *The Band Wagon* (1953) •628

A mystery more dark than any propounded by the film: why does Hitchcock persist in using actors as unattractively untalented as Robert Cummings? **Pauline Kael on Hitchcock's *Dial M for Murder*** (1953) •629

Cecil B. de Mille
Rather against his will,
Was persuaded to leave Moses
Out of The War of the Roses.

Nicholas Bentley on Hollywood impresario C.B. de Mille •630

Charlton Heston has a bad memory.
He still thinks he's Moses parting the Red Sea.

Barbara Stanwyck •631

A man who can part the Red Sea but apparently not his own hairpiece.

Dick Vosburgh and Denis King on Charlton Heston; *Beauty and the Beards* (2001) •632

Marilyn Monroe was good at playing abstract confusion in the same way that a midget is good at being short.

Clive James •633

She has breasts of granite and a mind like a Gruyere cheese.

Billy Wilder on Marilyn Monroe •634

A vacuum with nipples.

Otto Preminger on Marilyn Monroe •635

It's like kissing Hitler.

Tony Curtis gives his verdict on kissing Marilyn Monroe;
A. Hunter, *Tony Curtis* (1985) •636

[Tony Curtis] only said that about kissing Hitler because I wore prettier dresses than he did.

Marilyn Monroe •637

I miss her. It was like going to the dentist, making a picture with her.

Billy Wilder on Monroe •638

Most of the time he sounds like he has a mouthful of wet toilet paper.

Rex Reed on Marlon Brando ·639

I have a face that would stop a sundial.

Charles Laughton ·640

I have a face like an elephants behind.

Charles Laughton ·641

If, sir, I possessed , as you suggest the power of conveying unlimited sexual attraction through the potency of my voice, I would not be reduced to accepting a miserable pittance from the BBC for interviewing a faded female in a damp basement.

Gilbert Harding's reply to Mae West's manager, who had asked 'Can't you sound a bit more sexy when you interview her?'. In S.Grenfell, *Gilbert Harding by his Friends* (1961) ·642

*The best time I ever had with Joan Crawford was when I pushed her down the stairs in **What Ever Happened to Baby Jane?***

Bette Davies ·643

She was good at what she did, at what she settled for.

Bette Davies on Joan Crawford ·644

Take away the pop eyes, the cigarette and those funny clipped words and what have you got?

Joan Crawford on her old chum, Bette Davies ·645

*You look at Ernest Borgnine
and you think to yourself:
was there anybody else
hurt in the accident?*

Don Rickles ·646

Mia Farrow? I always knew Frank would end up in bed with a boy.

Ava Gardner is disparaging about ex-husband Frank Sinatra's latest squeeze ·647

*The rudest man I ever met, and
unattractive — pock-marked as
an Easter Island statue.*

Broadcaster Libby Purves on Richard Burton ·648

*Her face could launch
a thousand dredgers.*

Jack De Manio on Glenda Jackson ·649

*You're so vain, you probably
think this song is about you.*

Carly Simon's song, reputedly about Warren Beatty ·650

Michael Caine can out-act any, well nearly any, telephone kiosk you care to mention.

Hugh Leonard, Irish playwright ·651

Michael Caine compares himself to Gene Hackman. This is foolish. Hackman is an intimidating and dangerous actor. Mr. Caine is about as dangerous as Laurel and Hardy, or indeed both, and as intimidating as Shirley Temple.

Richard Harris ·652

He has the attention span of a bolt of lightning.

Robert Redford on *Butch Cassidy...* co-star Paul Newman ·653

Robert Redford has turned almost alarmingly blond — he's gone past platinum, he must be into plutonium; his hair is co-ordinated with his teeth. **Pauline Kael, 1976 ·654**

Poor little man. They made him out of lemon Jell-O and there he is.

Adela Rogers St John on Robert Redford ·655

To know her is not necessarily to love her.

Rex Reed on notorious 'diva' Barbra Streisand ·656

He is to acting what Liberace was to pumping iron.

Rex Reed on Sylvester Stallone ·657

You thought Dirk Benedict had problems in TV's Battlestar Galactica? In Scavenger Hunt, he really had problems — in one mercifully brief scene, he was out-acted by a jock-strap.

Rona Barrett on Dirk Benedict ·658

What do you mean, heart attack? You've got to have a heart before you can have an attack.

Billy Wilder on Peter Sellers' coronary ·659

Trying for the mystery of glamour, Julie Andrews merely coarsens her shining nice-girl image, becoming a nasty Girl Guide. **Pauline Kael** ·660

Like Dionysus crossed with a convent girl on her first bender.

Pauline Kael assesses Prince's performance in *Purple Rain;* in *The New Yorker,* August 1984 ·661

I once described him as a brown condom full of walnuts.

Clive James on Arnold Schwarzenegger; in *Daily Mail* August 2003 ·662

A fellow with the inventiveness of Albert Einstein but with the attention span of Daffy Duck.

Tom Shales on Robin Williams ·663

Demi Moore is the Arnold Schwarzenegger of women.

Candace Bushnell ·664

*Ken Russell casts himself in the title role of his own film, **The Secret Life of Arnold Bax**, and gives a portrayal so dire that I suspect he may have had to perform sexual favours for himself on the casting couch in order to get the part.*

Victor Lewis-Smith ·665

It's a new low for actresses when you have to wonder what's between her ears instead of her legs.

Katherine Hepburn, after Sharon Stone's infamous leg-uncrossing, sans knickers, in *Basic Instinct* ·666

Jean-Claude van Damme exudes the charisma of a packet of Cup-a-Soup. **Jonathan Romney** ·667

It is like kissing the Berlin Wall.

Helena Bonham Carter on acting with Woody Allen ·668

All my life I wanted to look like Liz Taylor. Now I find that Liz Taylor is beginning to look like me.

Drag queen Divine ·669

Elizabeth Taylor's so fat, she puts mayonnaise on aspirin.

Joan Rivers ·670

On being asked at a press conference how it felt to act with a screen legend like Nicole Kidman: She's not a legend, she's a beginner. You can't be a legend at whatever age she is.

The truly legendary Lauren Bacall; in *Observer* August 2000 ·671

Jack Warner has oilcloth pockets so he can steal soup.

Wilson Mizner ·672

I think that's what they call professional courtesy.

Herman J. Mankiewicz, on hearing that a Hollywood agent had swum safely in shark-infested waters; attrib. ·673

The only Greek Tragedy I know.

Billy Wilder on Spyros Skouras, Head of Fox Studios; attrib., perhaps apocryphal ·674

Do you have any idea how bad the picture is?
I'll tell you. Stay away from the neighbourhood
where it's playing — don't even go near that street!
It might rain — you could get caught in a downpour,
and to keep dry you'd have to go inside the theatre.

Herman J. Mankiewicz, attrib. ·675

Slimelight

Long-serving *New Yorker* film critic
Pauline Kael, on Chaplin's *Limelight* (1952) ·676

I would like to recommend this film to those
who can stay interested in Ronald Colman's
amnesia for two hours and who could with
pleasure eat a bowl of Yardley's shaving
soap for breakfast. **James Agee, reviewing *Random Harvest,* (1942)** ·677

So mincing as to border on baby talk.

Bosley Crowther on *It's A Wonderful Life* (1946) •678

Several tons of dynamite are set off in this picture; none of it under the right people.

James Agee finds fault with *Tycoon* (1947); **in *The Nation*,** February 1948 •679

The old master has turned out another Hitchcock and bull story, in which the mystery is not so much who done it as who cares. **Time magazine on Hitchcock's *Vertigo*** (1958) •680

*The only really satisfactory way to dispose
of **Peeping Tom** would be to shovel it up
and flush it swiftly down the nearest sewer.
Even then, the stench would remain.*

Derek Hill on *Peeping Tom* (1960) ·681

Let my people go!

Mort Sahl at a viewing of *Exodus* (1960); **attrib.** 1961·682

*They only got two things right
in **Lawrence of Arabia**: the
camels and the sand.* Lowell Thomas (1962) ·683

*I had never numbered Bergman among
the slyer contemporary wags; all the same,
I expected something slightly less elephantine
than tinted Norman Wisdom. What goings-on!
I gape in amazement, remarks one of the
subtitles, and I can't say I blame it.*

**Kenneth Tynan on Ingmar Bergman film
*Now About These Women*** (1964) ·684

*This dingy charade spends two hours repeating
a message already familiar in the first twenty
minutes: All they want is my body. Carroll Baker
supplies the body, if not the erotic incandescence
that made them want it. She didn't die of
pneumonia, says her agent after the girl gasps
her last, she died of life. In fact, she died of
neither. Nothing reveals the essential mendacity
of Harlow more clearly than its refusal to admit
that a Hollywood sex symbol could die of uremic
poisoning. Angela Lansbury, Raf Vallone, and
Red Buttons are among those who officiate
at this shoddy exhumation.* **Kenneth Tynan on a 1965 'biopic'
of Hollywood actress Jean Harlow ·685**

*The nuns, as always in American films, are average
American housewives inexplicably veiled in black;
a twinkling bunch of good-hearted gossips, healthily
unconcerned with sex. They sing all their wimples off,
including — strangely enough — the Mother Superior,
who bursts into full contralto shortly after informing
us that singing in the cloister is forbidden.*

Kenneth Tynan on *The Sound of Music* (1965) ·686

Mister Moses is the one about the African village that must either quit its ancestral home to accommodate the new dam or stay and get drowned. Like most films, it stars Carroll Baker. The running time is 115 minutes; the walking-out time is much earlier. The weather throughout is excellent.

Kenneth Tynan on *Mister Moses* (1965) ·687

Wasn't there perhaps one little Von Trapp who didn't want to sing his head off, or who screamed that he wouldn't act out little glockenspiel routines for Papa's party guests, or who got nervous and threw up if he had to get on stage?

Wishful thinking from Pauline Kael as she reviews *The Sound of Music* (1965) ·688

Then came *Easy Rider,* a disaster in the history of film...

David Thomson, critic, on *Easy Rider* (1969) ·689

The movie is of an unbelievable badness; it brings back clichés you didn't know you knew… You can't get angry at something this stupefying; it seems to have been made by trolls. Pauline Kael on *Song of Norway,* a biopic of composer Edvard Grieg, (1970) •690

I still can't believe I saw this freak show, a self-consciously mod, disjointed patchwork of leers, vulgarity, and general ineptness.
William Wolf on *Myra Breckenridge*, in *Cue,* (1970) •691

If I was the ghost of Marilyn Monroe and had a few good friends high up in the councils of the Society of Psychical Research, I think I might sue for defamation of ectoplasm.
Benny Green, on *Goodbye, Norma Jean* (1975) in *Punch,*
October 1976 •692

The jokes are tired and can often be seen dragging their feet towards us a mile off; when they finally arrive, we are more apt to commiserate than laugh.

John Simon on Woody Allen's *Annie Hall* (1977) ·693

To be fair, the movie does show a certain charm in its relentlessly stupid grasp of the obvious. When Frampton sings **The Long and Winding Road,** *for example, he is walking down a long and winding road. You keep laughing and thinking it can't get any worse. But it does.* Charles M. Young on Beatles movie ***Sgt. Pepper's Lonely Hearts Club Band*** (1978) **in *Rolling Stone* magazine** ·694

Table for Five *would be an ideal movie to watch on a plane; at least they provide free sick bags.*

Simon Rose reviews *Table for Five* (1983) •695

The picture is like a slightly psychopathic version of an old Saturday-afternoon serial, with Harry sneering at the scum and cursing them before he shoots them with his king-size custom-made 44 Auto Mag. He (Clint Eastwood) takes particular pleasure in kicking and bashing a foul-mouthed lesbian; we get the idea. In his eyes, she's worse than her male associates, becuase women are supposed to be ladies. Eastwood's disapproval of her impropriety sits a little bit oddly in a movie with sub-barnyard jokes about a little bulldog's hindquarters and a laugh-fest centering on a man shot in the genitals and a frankfurter covered in ketchup.

Pauline Kael on *Sudden Impact* (1983)**, in *The New Yorker*,** January 1984 •696

*What kind of a title for a movie is **Greystoke: The Legend of Tarzan, Lord of the Apes?** A pompous, foolish one. There can't be many people who will remember this title, or many theatres that are equipped with colons for their marquees, either.* **Pauline Kael on *Greystoke...*** (1983)in ***The New Yorker,*** April 1984 ·697

Makes you look for something lighter and wittier such as a documentary on the Khmer Rouge.

Simon Rose on *Shanghai Surprise* (1986) ·698

A wet piece of kitsch.

Pauline Kael on *Rain Man* (1988) ·699

Here is the ideal date movie, assuming you're dating a psychopath sadist with a high tolerance for dilly-dallying... The younger actors all seem fresh off the campus of the James Woods-Willem Dafoe Institute For Acting Surly, Nervous and Dishevelled.

Ralph Novak on *Reservoir Dogs* (1991) ·700

What did I think of **Titanic?** I'd rather have been on it.

Miles Kruger assesses 1997's *Titanic* ·701

Proof, if proof were needed, that the return of the dumb teen comedy genre may be on its last legs, Danny Leiner's woefully inept buddy flick redefines unfunny in ways you never knew possible. Mistaking repetition of dialogue for a fruitful means of laughter grabbing, the misadventures of the two stoners searching aimlessly for their missing motor takes in charmless, witless, and painfully dull in equal measures, without ever throwing in an original idea in its 82-minute running time.

Risible, dire, or just about any synonym for Godawful you want to come up with… This unmitigated stream of celluloid ordure could draw a chalk outline round its corpse. All together: 'Dude, where's my refund?'

William Thomas on *Dude, Where's My Car?* (2000)
In *Empire* magazine, March 2001 ·702

No intelligent person could like this film.

Andrew O'Hagan, of *The Daily Telegraph,* on *Pearl Harbour* (2001). He's not wrong ·703

It's… possible that the world would be a better place if no one went to see **Collateral Damage** *(Warner Bros.)… it's another dumb vengeance picture —* **In the Bedroom** *for meatheads.*

David Edelstein on *Collateral Damage* (2001), in *Slate,* February 2002 ·704

EGO LIKE A RAGING TOOTH

My dear, good is not the word.

Max Beerbohm, 'reassuring' a leading lady after a particularly bad first night; attrib. ·705

Go on failing. Go on. Only next time, try to fail better.

Samuel Beckett finds a use for advice given in his 1983 play Westward Ho ("Ever tried. Ever failed. No matter. Try again. Fail again. Fail better") when during a rehearsal at the Royal Court an actor lamented, "I'm failing"; in Tony Richardson, *Long Distance Runner* (1993) •706

> *That popular Stage-playes… are all sinful, heathenish, lewde, ungodly Spectacles, and most pernicious Corruptions; condemned in all ages, as intolerable Mischiefes to Churches, to Republickes, to the manners, mindes, and soules of men. And that the Profession of Play-poets, of Stage-players; together with the penning, acting, and frequenting of Stage-playes, are unlawful, infamous, and misbeseeming Christians.*
>
> **William Prynne** (c.1600-1669) •707

Mr Ainley played the old codger like a toastmaster celebrating his golden wedding.

James Agate on Henry Ainley as Prospero,
1934 •708

An ego like a raging tooth.

W.B. Yeats on actress Mrs Patrick Campbell ·709

It is greatly to Mrs Patrick Campbell's credit that, bad as the play was, her acting was worse. It was a masterpiece of failure. **George Bernard Shaw on Mrs Patrick Campbell ·710**

She's such a nice woman. If you knew her you'd even admire her acting.

Mrs Patrick Campell on a fellow actress; recorded in James Agate's *diary* **6 May 1937 ·711**

Such a clever actress. Pity she does her hair with Bovril.

Mrs Patrick Campbell on a rival actress; in *Ned Sherrin in his Anecdotage* (1993); attrib. ·712

All through the five acts... he played the King as though under momentary apprehension that someone else was about to play the Ace.

Eugene Field, reviewing Creston Clarke's King Lear, *Denver Tribune,* 1880 ·713

I'm amazed he was such a good shot.

Noël Coward, on hearing that his accountant had blown his brains out;
in *Ned Sherrin's Theatrical Anecdotes* (1991) ·714

A women whose face looked as if it had been made of sugar and someone had licked it.

George Bernard Shaw on Isadora Duncan ·715

Tranquilized benevolence cascading from a great height, like royalty opening a bazaar.

Kenneth Tynan on Edith Evans in *All's Well That Ends Well*, 1959 ·716

*I have been looking around for an appropriate
wooden gift and am pleased hereby to present you
with Elsie Ferguson's performance in her new play.*

**Alexander Woollcott sends a congratulatory telegram for
George S. Kaufman's fifth wedding anniversary;
Howard Teichmann, *George S. Kaufman* (1973) ·717**

> *With his full mane of curly hair and
> dressed in a gold-encrusted tightly
> fitting mini-skirted costume, he
> struck me as more of an overweight
> elf than the savage conqueror of Asia.*

Arthur Thirkell on Albert Finney in *Tamberlaine,* 1976 ·718

*Finney's roughneck Hamlet is no prince at all,
let alone a sweet prince. More of a Spamlet really.*

Jason Hillgate on Albert Finney's performance at the Old Vic, 1975. In *Theatre* ·719

Onc critic complained that I had only two gestures — left hand up, and right hand down. What did he expect me to do? Bring out my prick?

John Gielgud ·720

Lillian Gish may be a charming person, but she is not Ophelia. She comes on stage as if she had been sent for to sew rings on the new curtains.

Mrs Patrick Campbell; in
Margot Peters, *Mrs Pat* (1984) ·721

Farley Granger played Mr. Darcy with all the flexibility of a telegraph pole.

Brooks Atkins, on Bo Goldman's musicial adaptation of *Pride and Prejudice* on Broadway in the 1950s ·722

Very good, very good. I always thought you would make an impression on the stage one day.

Sir William Schewnk Gilbert, to prima donna actress Henrietta Hodson, after she sat down and missed the chair. ·723

Mrs Holden acting his wife entered in a hurry crying "Oh my dear Count.' She inadvertently left out the 'o' in the pronunciation of the word count, giving it a vehement accent, put the house into such a laughter that London Bridge at low tide was silence to it.

An early review (1708) **of Mrs Holden as Lady Capulet in *Romeo and Juliet* ·724**

Miss Hunnicutt's Viola was not Patience on a Monument — it was a monument of patience.

Bernard Levin on Gayle Hunnicutt as Viola in *Twelfth Night* ·725

If they'd stuffed the child's head up the horse's arse, they would have solved two problems at once.

Noël Coward, referring to a performance starring child actress Bonnie Langford and a horse after the latter defecated on stage ·726

Geraldine McEwan, powdered white like a clownish, whey-faced doll simpered, whined and groaned to such effect as the Queen, that Edward's homosexuality became both understandable and forgivable.

Milton Shulman on a production of Brecht's *Edward II* ·727

Anna Neagle playing Queen Victoria always made me think that Albert must have married beneath him.

Noël Coward, in Sheridan Morley, *The Quotable Noël Coward* (1999) ·728

He delivers every line with a monotonous tenor bark as if addressing an audience of deaf Eskimos… It was P.G. Wodehouse who memorably said that the 'Tomorrow and tomorrow and tomorrow' speech has got a lot of spin on it but, as delivered by Mr. O'Toole, it is hit for six like a full toss. Michael Billington reviews Peter O'Toole as *Macbeth* in 1980 in *The Guardian* ·729

Denis Quilley played the role with all the charm and animation of the leg of a billiard table.

Bernard Levin on Denis Quilley as Charles Condamine in *High Spirits* (a musical version of Noël Coward's *Blithe Spirit*) ·730

He has taken to ambling across our stages, in a special, shell-shocked manner, choosing odd moments to jump and frisk, like a man through whom an electric current is being intermittently passed. **Kenneth Tynan on Ralph Richardson in *The White Carnation* by R.C. Sheriff ·731**

Ralph Richardson's Uncle Vanya is just his Falstaff with a hangover.

George Jean Nathan, US critic, 1946 ·732

Diana Rigg is built like a brick mausoleum with insufficient flying buttresses.

John Simon reviews Diana Rigg in a 1970 production of *Abelard and Heloise;* in Diana Rigg, *No Turn Unstoned* (1982) ·733

She was so dramatic she stabbed the potatoes at dinner.

Sydney Smith enhances actress Sarah Siddons' reputation for melodrama ·734

Mr. Torn allows words to revolve wanly in his mouth like a jingling key chain in a bored man's pocket.

John Simon on Rip Torn's performance in *Daughter of Silence; Music Box,* November 1961 ·735

Do you know how they are going to decide the Shakespeare-Bacon dispute? They are going to dig up Shakespeare and dig up Bacon; they are going to set their coffins side by side, and then they are going to get Tree to recite Hamlet to them and the one who turns in his coffin will be the author of the play.

W.S. Gilbert on actor Sir Herbert Beerbohm Tree ·736

There is no point in seeing a man reduced to hysterical panic if hysterical panic is his forte.

Michael Billington on Kenneth Williams in the farce, *Signed and Sealed* ·737

As swashbuckling Cyrano, Mr Woodward's performance buckles more often than it swashes.

Kenneth Hurren, *The Spectator,* 1970 ·738

He is an old bore. Even the grave yawns for him.

Herbert Beerbohm Tree, of actor Israel Zangwill; in Max Beerbohm, *Herbert Beerbohm Tree* (1920) ·739

The Syphilis and gonorrhoea of the theatre.
David Mamet on Frank Rich and John Simon, critics ·740

Review in a London newspaper of *A Good Time*, a show running at the Duchess Theatre in the early 1900s ·741

He gives the impression that he is a Rotarian
pork bucther about to tell the stalls a dirty story.

Felix Barker on Anthony Hopkins as Macbeth, 1973 ·742

This is the kind of show that gives pornography a bad name.

Clive Barnes on *Oh Calcutta!*, 1969 ·743

The Elder Statesman is a zombie play designed for the living dead.

Alan Brien on T.S. Eliot's play; in *The Spectator*, September 1958 ·744

The Birthday Party is like a vintage Hitchcock thriller which has been, in the immortal tear-stained words of Orson Welles, edited by a cross-eyed studio janitor with a lawn-mower.

Alan Brien reviews Harold Pinter's play in *The Spectator*, May 1958 ·745

Am sitting in the smallest room of my house.
Your review is before me. In a moment, it will
be behind me. Noël Coward, apocryphal ·746

*At the beginning of **Hamlet** the stage looks like a Build-Your-Own-Elsinore kit.*

Robert Cushman in the *Observer*, 1981 ·747

Shut up, Arnold, or I'll direct
this play the way you wrote it!

John Dexter, to the playwright Arnold Wesker;
in *Ned Sherrin in his Anecdotage* (1993) ·748

The real complexity of life among Mr. Lonsdale's powerfully sexed
grammarians can be indicated in a sentence, though a tough one:
Michael, engaged to Molly, is really in love with Diana, whom he
seduced once in Paris; George can't decide whether to marry Celia
or Maggie, both of whom he has seduced here and there at various
times; and Elsie, though married to Reggie, is still strongly attracted
to her first husband, John, who has seduced practically everybody and
likes to talk about it. Anyway, all these people, along with a drunken
butler and an old family lawyer, both standard models, are visible
on the stage, sometimes at once. **Wolcott Gibbs on *Another Love Story***
by Frederick Lonsdale. From *Seasons in*
***the Sun & Other Pleasures* (1946) ·749**

Having decided to focus on the hole rather than the doughnut, as it were, Ensler happily disappears up it. Germaine Greer on Eve Ensler's *The Vagina Monologues;* in the *Daily Telegraph,* March 2002 •750

I want something to keep me awake thinking it was the food I ate and not the show I saw.

George S. Kaufman after a disastrous preview; in Howard Teichmann, *George S. Kaufmann* (1973) •751

*If a director doesn't want to do **The Shrew**, this is a pretty good way not to do it.*

Stanley Kaufmann on the American Conservatory Theater's production of Shakespeare's *The Taming of the Shrew,* December 1973 •752

There was laughter in the back of the theatre, leading to the belief that someone was telling jokes back there.

George S. Kaufman; in Howard Teichmann, *George S. Kaufman* (1973) •753

… Its like is rarely met with except on a fishmonger's slab, and now I feel very ill indeed, and would like to lie down.

Bernard Levin on *The Amorous Prawn,* 1959 ·754

I think I'll go by boat.

Bernard Levin on *Boeing Boeing* by Marc Camoletti ·755

On its face value, it is callous and empty enough: what lies in its Freudian depths one dreads to think.

Anthony Seymour on Pinter's *The Homecoming,* in the *Yorkshire Post* June 1965 ·756

The plot is of such titanic and recondite imbecility that I couldn't reveal it if I wanted to…

Most of the dialogue consists of members of the cast explaining the plot to one another, a service I can well imagine they need.

But I cannot see that they need the explanations to be couched in language of such shattering banality.

Bernard Levin in the *Daily Express* on William Fairchild's *The Sound of Murder,* August 1959 ·757

The pitiful little thing has to do with horse racing, and you might perhaps say that it is by Imbecility out of Staggering Incompetence. Bernard Levin on *Dazzling Prospect* by M.J. Farrell and John Perry; in the *Daily Express,* June 1961 ·758

I didn't like the play, but then I saw it under adverse conditions — the curtain was up.

Groucho Marx; ad-lib, attributed in an interview by Marx to
George S. Kaufman; Peter Hay, *Broadway Anecdotes* (1989) ·759

…the co-sponsors of this project […] laid down a barrage of dust: dirty costumes which seemed to have been bought complete from a theatrical warehouse flapped across the stage, wildly reciting lines. Mary McCarthy, February 1947 ·760

For all its frenzied breast-beating, this is a show with about as much heart as the Tin Man in The Wizard of Oz.

Charles Osborne on West End musical *Miss Saigon*. In *First Nights, Second Thoughts* (2001) ·761

All my envy goes to the inspired Mr. Walter Winchell, who walked wanly out into the foyer after the third act — there are four acts and they are long, long acts — and summed up the whole thing in the phrase, Well, for Chrichton out loud!

Dorothy Parker, in the *New Yorker*, reviewing the Broadway opening of J.M. Barrie's play *The Admirable Chrichton* ·762

It aims at being a despairing cry but achieves only the stature of a self-pitying snivel.

Milton Shulman on John Osborne's *Look Back In Anger* ·763

The Cigarette Girl certainly made me gasp in amazement, it is so unbelievably bad. …The dialogue is putrid, the acting early marionette, the evening disastrous. **Arthur Thirkell on *The Cigarette Girl* by William Douglas Home,** 1962 ·764

The play grated on me like the sustained whine of an ancient tramcar coming down a steep hill.

J.C. Trewin reviews John Osborne's *Look Back in Anger* in *The London Illustrated News*, May 1956 ·765

Once upon a time there was an actor called gruff Laurence Olivier, whose wife was an actress called pert Vivien Leigh, and a playwright called clever Terence Rattigan wrote a play for them called **The Sleeping Prince**, *with a gruff part for him and a pert part for her, and to nobody's surprise it ran happily ever after, with twice-weekly matinées… Among the select group of plays written for eminent husband-and-wife teams in coronation years, it ranks very high…*

Kenneth Tynan in the *Daily Sketch,* November 1953 ·766

When you've seen all of Ionesco's plays, I felt at the end, you've seen one of them.

Kenneth Tynan, after seeing *Victims of Duty* by Eugène Ionesco, 1960 ·767

OPIUM GLAZED EYES AND RAT-TAILY HAIR

Fredrick Leighton: *My dear Mr Whistler, you leave your pictures in such a sketchy, unfinished state. Why don't you ever finish them?*[768]

James Whistler: *My dear Leighton, why do you ever begin yours?*[769]

It resembles a tortoise-shell cat having a fit in a plate of tomatoes.

Mark Twain on J.M.W. Turner's *The Slave Ship* ·770

It makes me look as if I were straining at a stool.

Winston Churchill on his portrait by Graham Sutherland ·771

The only genius with an IQ of 60.

Gore Vidal on Andy Warhol ·772

Skill without imagination is craftsmanship and gives us many useful objects such as wickerwork picnic baskets. Imagination without skill gives us modern art.

Tom Stoppard, *Artist Descending a staircase*, BBC Radio, 1972 ·773

Jeff Koons' work is the last bit of methane left in the intestine of the dead cow that is post-modernism.

Time magazine's Robert Hughes on sculptor Jeff Koons ·774

When I look at these works, 'culture' only makes me think of yoghurt.

Edna Weiss, Royal Academian, on the Turner Prize shortlist ·775

Quill, n. An implement of torture yielded by a goose and commonly wielded by an ass…

Ambrose Bierce, *The Devil's Dictionary* (1911) •776

Curse the blasted, jelly-boned swines, the slimy, the belly-wriggling invertebrates, the miserable sodding rotters, the flaming sods, the snivelling, dribbling, palsied, pulseless lot that make up England today. They've got white of egg in their veins, and their spunk is that watery it's a marvel they can breed.

D.H. Lawrence on those critics and readers who failed to appreciate him •777

A critic is a person who will slit the throat of a skylark to see what makes it sing.

J.M. Synge ·778

Asking a playwright how he felt about critics was like asking a lamppost how it felt about dogs. Christopher Hampton, in *The Times* April 1995 ·779

Critics are like eunuchs in a harem; they know how it's done, they've seen it done every day, but they're unable to do it themselves.

Brendan Behan ·780

I never read a book before reviewing it — it prejudices a man so.

Sydney Smith, (1771-1845), clergyman and wit ·781

A louse in the locks of literature.

Alfred, Lord Tennyson isn't a fan of critic John Churton Collins; in Evan Charteris, 'Life and Letters of Sir Edmund Gosse' (1931) ·782

After all, one knows one's weak points so well, that it's rather bewildering to have the critics overlook them and invent others.

Edith Wharton, *letter*, 19 November 1909 ·783

*A critic is a man who knows
the way but can't drive the car.*

Kenneth Tynan, in *New York Times Magazine*
9 January 1966 ·784

*There is, perhaps, no more dangerous man in the world
than the man with the sensibilities of an artist but without
creative talent. With luck such men make wonderful theatrical
impresarios and interior decorators, or else they become mass
murderers or critics.* **Barry Humphries, *More Please*** (1992) ·785

*Thou eunuch of language… thou pimp
of gender… murderous accoucheur of
infant learning… thou pickle-herring
in the puppet show of nonsense.*

Scots poet Robert Burns on an anonymous critic ·786

*Last night I dined out in Chelsea, and mauled
the dead and rotten carcases of several works
written by my friends.* **Virginia Woolf** ·787

*Your critic has cleared himself of the charge of personal
malice… but he has only done so by a tacit admission that
he has really no critical instinct about literature and literary
work, which, in one who writes about literature, is, I need
hardly say, a much graver fault than malice of any kind.*
Oscar Wilde, *In Defence of Dorian Gray* (1891) ·788

An editor is one who separates the wheat from the chaff and prints the chaff.

Adlai Stevenson, *The Stevenson Wit* (1966) ·789

Some of the editors wrote rejection slips that were more creative than anything I had written. On my tenth submission to Redbook… "Mrs Clark, your stories are light, slight, and trite." My first novella was returned with the succinct note: "We found the heroine as boring as her husband had."

Mary Higgins Clark, in *The Writing Life: Collection* from *Washington Post Book World* (2003) ·790

Scribbler, n. A professional writer whose views are antagonistic to one's own.

Ambrose Bierce, *The Devil's Dictionary* (1911) ·791

The media. It sounds like a convention of spiritualists.

Tom Stoppard ·792

The fact that a man is a newspaper reporter is evidence of some flaw of character.

Lyndon B Johnson ·793

Lickspittle, n.
A useful functionary,
not infrequently found
editing a newspaper…
Ambrose Bierce, *The Devil's Dictionary*
(1911) ·794

There is nothing at
all the matter with
some journalists
that a quick slap
in the face couldn't
sort out. Elvis Costello (1995) ·795

David Frost has
risen without a trace.
Kitty Muggeridge on journalist and interviewer
David Frost; in conversation with Malcolm
Muggeridge c. 1965. ·796

So boring you fall asleep
halfway through her name.
Alan Bennett on Arianna Stassinopoulos (now
Arianna Huffington) in the *Observer* ·797

A one-man slum.
An anonymous commentator on American journalist Heywood Broun (1888-1939) ·798

Muggeridge, a garden gnome expelled from Eden, has come to rest as a gargoyle brooding over a derelict cathedral.

Kenneth Tynan on Malcolm Muggeridge ·799

A legend in his own lunchtime.

David Climie, of Dennis Main Wilson; also attrib. to Christopher Wordsworth of Clifford Makins ·801

I cannot take seriously the criticism of someone who doesn't know how to use a semi-colon.

Shirley Conran on Julie Burchill ·800

Books are not made like children but like pyramids… and they're just as useless! And they stay in the desert!… Jackals piss at their feet and the bourgeois climb up on them.

Gustave Flaubert, *letter to Ernest Feydeau*, 1857 ·802

There are books of which the backs and covers are by far the best parts.

Charles Dickens ·803

*The more I read him, the less
I wonder that they poisoned him.*

Lord Macaulay on Socrates ·804

Plato is a bore.

Friedrich Nietzsche ·805

A Methodist parson in Bedlam.

Horace Walpole on Dante ·806

*The swish-swash of the press,
the bum of impudency, the
shambles of beastliness…
the toadstool of the realm.*

**Gabriel Harvey on 16th Century pamphleteer
and playwright Thomas Nashe** ·807

*This dodipoule, this didpopper… why, thou
arrant butter whoe, thou coteueane and
scrattop of scoldes, will thou never leave
affecting a dead Carcasse… a wispe, a wispe,
rippe, rippe, you kitchen-stuff wrangler!*

Thomas Nashe, on Gabriel Harvey ·808

With the single exception of Homer, there is no eminent writer, not even Sir Walter Scott, whom I can despise so entirely as I despise Shakespeare when I measure my mind against his.

George Bernard Shaw in *Saturday Review*
September 1896 ·809

Having never had any mental vision, he has now lost his bodily sight; a silly coxcomb, fancying himself a beauty; an unclean beast, with nothing more human about him than his guttering eyelids; the fittest doom for him would be to hang him on the highest gallows, and set his head on the Tower of London.

Salmasius (Claude de Saumaise) on blind poet John Milton ·810

This obscure, this eccentric, and disgusting poem.

Voltaire, on John Milton's epic poem *Paradise Lost* ·811

Doth that lewd harlot,
  that poetic queen,
Famed through White Friars,
  you know who I mean,
Mend for reproof, others set
  up in spight,
To flux, take glisters, vomits,
  purge and write.
Long with a sciatica she's
  beside lame,
Her limbs distortured,
  nerves shrunk up with pain,
And therefore I'll all sharp
  reflections shun,
Poverty, poetry, pox are plagues
  enough for one.

Anonymous, *The Epistle of Julian*
(published 1687), **referring to Restoration
playwright Aphra Behn** ·812

*It is a pretty poem, Mr Pope,
but you must not call it Homer.*

**Richard Bentley, when pressed by Pope to
comment on *'My Homer'*, i.e. Pope's translation of the *Iliad.* In John Hawkins (ed.), *The
Works of Samuel Johnson*** (1787) ·813

*A monster gibbering
shrieks, and gnashing
imprecations against
mankind — tearing
down all shreds of
modesty, past all
sense of manliness and
shame; filthy in word,
filthy in thought, furious,
raging, obscene.*

**William Makepeace Thackeray
on Jonathan Swift, author of
*Gulliver's Travels*** ·814

I do not think this poem will reach its destination.

Voltaire on Jean-Baptiste Rousseau's
Ode To Posterity ·815

Gibbon's style is detestable, but it is not the worst thing about him. Samuel Taylor Coleridge
on Edward Gibbon ·818

*I'm glad you'll write,
You'll furnish paper when I shite.*

Lady Mary Wortley Montagu (1689-1762),
'Reasons that Induced Dr S- to write a Poem
called the *'Lady's Dressing Room'* ·816

Very nice, though there are dull stretches.

Antoine de Rivarol on a two-line poem ·819

Thomas Gray walks as if he had fouled his small-clothes, and looks as if he smelt it.

Christopher Smart, of fellow poet
Thomas Gray ·817

A philosophising servant… that hyena in petticoats.

Horace Walpole on Mary Wollstonecraft,
Letters, 1798 ·820

How thankful we ought to be that Wordsworth was only a poet and not a musician. Fancy a symphony by Wordsworth! Fancy having to sit it out! And fancy what it would have been if he had written fugues!

Samuel Butler (1835-1902), *Notebooks* (1912) ·821

An Archangel a little damaged.

Charles Lamb on Samuel Taylor Coleridge, *letter to Wordsworth,* 26 April 1816 ·823

It is long yet vigorous, like the penis of a jackass.

Sydney Smith on an article in the *Edinburgh Review* **by Henry Brougham** ·824

There are the old raptures about mountains and cataracts; the old flimsy philosophy about the effect of scenery upon the mind; the old crazy, mystical metaphysics; the endless wilderness of dull, flat, prosaic twaddle; and here and there fine descriptions and energetic declamations interspersed.

Thomas Babington Macaulay on William Wordsworth, *journal entry,* July 1850 ·822

What a hideous, odd-looking man Sydney Smith is. With a mouth like an oyster and three double chins

Mrs Brookfield, on the Reverend Sydney Smith ·825

On Waterloo's ensanguined plain
Full many a gallant man was slain,
But none, by sabre or by shot,
Fell half so flat as Walter Scott.

**Anonymous, of Scott's poem
'The Field of Waterloo'** (1815) ·826

Of Jane Austen: It seems a great pity that they allowed her to die a natural death.

Mark Twain; in Alex Ayres (ed.), *The Wit and Wisdom of Mark Twain* (2005) ·827

*The Edinburgh praises Jack Keats or Ketch or whatever
his names are; — why his is the Onanism of poetry.*

**Lord Byron finds a self-indulgent streak in the work of fellow poet John Keats;
in *a letter to his publisher John Murray,*** 4 November 1820 ·828

*I see a schoolboy when I think of him
With face and nose pressed to a sweet-shop window,
For certaily he sank into his grave
His senses and his heart unsatisfied,
And made - being poor, ailing and ignorant,
Shut out from all the luxury of the world,
The ill-bred son of a livery stable-keeper-
Luxuriant song.*

**W.B. Yeats qualifies his praise of Keats,
'Ego Dominus Tuus'** (1917) ·829

Always looking at himself in mirrors to make sure he was sufficiently outrageous.

Enoch Powell on Lord Byron, *Sunday Times* May 1988 ·830

I never heard a single expression of fondness for him fall from the lips of any of those who knew him well. **Lord Macaulay on Lord Byron,** *letter* 7 June 1831 ·831

Mad, bad, and dangerous to know.

Lady Charles Lamb's assessment, in her diary, of Lord Byron after their first meeting at a ball in March 1812 ·832

The world is rid of Lord Bryon, but the deadly slime of his touch still remains.

John Constable, artist, on news of Bryon's death ·833

*He is a person of very epic appearance — and has
a fine head as far as the outside goes — and wants
nothing but taste to make the inside equally attractive.*

Lord Byron, of poet and writer Robert Southey; *letter,* 30 September 1813 ·834

*Mr. Southey wades through the ponderous volumes
of travels and old chronicles, from which he carefully
selects all that is false, useless and absurd, as being
essentially poetical; and when he has a commonplace
book full of monstrosities, strings them into an epic.*

Thomas Love Peacock on the British poet laureate Robert Southey,
in *The Four Ages of Poetry,* (1820) ·835

Our opinion then is this: that Barère approached nearer than any person mentioned in history or fiction, whether man or devil, to the idea of consummate and universal depravity. In him the qualities which are the proper objects of contempt, preserve an exquisite and absolute harmony. When we put everything together, sensuality, poltroonery, baseness, effrontery, mendacity, barbarity, the result is something which in a novel we should condemn as caricature, and to which, we venture to say, no parallel can be found in history.

Thomas Babington, Lord Macaulay, reviewing the memoirs of French revolutionary Bertrand Barère, in a passage once described as the most sustained piece of invective in the English language ·836

A great cow full of ink.

Gustave Flaubert on George Sand ·837

At bottom, this Macaulay is but a poor creature with his dictionary literature and erudition, his saloon arrogance. He has no vision in him. He will neither see nor do anything great. **Thomas Carlyle on Thomas Babington Macaulay** ·838

I wish her characters would talk a little less like the heroes and heroines of police reports.

George Eliot, on *Jane Eyre* by Charlotte Brontë ·839

A dirty man with opium-glazed eyes and rat-taily hair.

Lady Frederick Cavendish on Alfred, Lord Tennyson ·840

He could not think up to the height of his own towering style.

G.K. Chesterton on Alfred, Lord Tennyson; *The Victorian Age in Literature* (1912) ·841

Longfellow is to poetry what the barrel-organ is to music.

Van Wyck Brooks on Henry Wadsworth Longfellow ·842

A large shaggy dog unchained scouring the beaches of the world and baying at the moon. Robert Louis Stevenson on Walt Whitman ·843

I could readily see in Emerson… a gaping flaw. It was the insinuation that had he lived in those days when the world was made, he might have offered some valuable suggestions.

Herman Melville on Ralph Waldo Emerson •844

Arnold is a dandy Isaiah, a poet without passion, whose verse, written in surplice, is for freshmen and for gentle maidens who will be wooed to the arms of these future rectors.

George Meredith on the poet and essayist Matthew Arnold, in *Fortnightly Review* July 1909 •845

Carlyle is a poet to whom nature has denied the faculty of verse.

Alfred, Lord Tennyson, *letter to W.E. Gladstone,* c.1870 •846

It was very good of God to let Carlyle and Mrs Carlyle marry one another and so make only two people miserable instead of four.

Samuel Butler, *letter to Miss E.M.A. Savage,* 21 November 1884 •847

The same old sausage, fizzing and sputtering in its own grease.

Henry James on Thomas Carlyle •848

I was never allowed to read the popular American children's books of my day because, as my mother said, the children spoke bad English without the author's knowing it. **Edith Wharton** •849

The original Greek is of great use in elucidating Browning's translation of the Agamemnon.

Robert Yelverton Tyrell's habitual remark to students;
in Ulick O'Connor, *Oliver St John Gogarty* (1964) ·850

A provinicial manufacturer of gauche and heavy fictions that sometimes have corresponding values.

Critic F.R. Leavis on Thomas Hardy ·851

No one has written worse English than Mr. Hardy in some of his novels — cumbrous, stilted, ugly, and inexpressive — yes. Virginia Woolf on Thomas Hardy,
The Moment, (1947) ·852

A little emasculated mass of inanity.

Theodore Roosevelt on Henry James ·853

Henry James has a mind so fine no idea could violate it.

T.S. Eliot ·854

I am reading Henry James…
and feel myself as one entombed
in a block of smooth amber.

Virginia Woolf on Henry James •855

The work of Henry James has
always seemed divisible by a
simple dynastic arrangement
into three reigns: James I,
James II, and the Old Pretender.

Philip Guadella, *Collected Essay, 'Men of Letters: Mr Henry James'*
(1920) •856

She plunged into a sea of platitudes, and with the
powerful breast stroke of a channel swimmer made
her way towards the white cliffs of the obvious.

W. Somerset Maugham, *A Writer's Notebook* (1949), written in 1892 •857

Concerning no subject would Shaw be deterred by the minor accident of total ignorance from penning a definitive opinion.

Roger Scruton on George Bernard Shaw ·858

On remarking that George Bernard Shaw's wife was a good listener:
God knows she's had plenty of practice. J.B. Priestley, *Margin Released* (1962) ·859

Silence — the most perfect expression of scorn. George Bernard Shaw,
Back to Methuselah, (1921).
If only he'd taken his own advice ·860

When you were a little boy somebody ought to have said hush just once.

Mrs Patrick Campbell, *letter to George Bernard Shaw,*
1 November 1912 ·861

Hugo — hélas! (Hugo — alas!)

André Gide, when asked who was the greatest 19th-century poet. In Claude Martin, *La Maturité d'André Gide* (1977) ·862

The human race, to which so many of my readers belong.

G. K. Chesterton ·863

Conrad spent a day finding the mot juste; then killed it.

Ford Madox Ford, in Robert Lowell, *Notebook 1967-68* (1969) ·864

What is Conrad but the wreck of Stevenson floating about in the slipsop of Henry James.

George Moore on the novelist Joseph Conrad. ·865

A jingo imperialist, morally insensitive and aesthetically disgusting.

George Orwell on Rudyard Kipling ·866

I have always thought it was a sound impulse by which he [Kipling] was driven to put his 'Recessional' into the waste-paper basket, and a great pity that Mrs Kipling fished it out and made him send it to The Times.

Max Beerbohm, *letter,* 30 October 1913 ·867

As a contribution to natural history the work is negligible.

E.V. Lucas in a review of Kenneth Grahame's *Wind in the Willows;* in *Times Literary Supplement* 22 October 1908 ·868

*I am also writing a preface for an American edition of Galsworthy's **Man of Property**. Ever read it? Don't. He was the last English novelist to be granted general reverence. He is really shockingly dull. I had the hope that it was youthful snobbery that made me despise him. But no. He's no good.*

Evelyn Waugh, in *a letter to Anne Fleming,* 7 August 1963. **From *The Letters of Evelyn Waugh*** (1980) ·869

E.M. Forster never gets any further than warming the teapot. He's a rare fine hand at that. Feel this teapot. Is it not beautifully warm? Yes, but there ain't going to be no tea. Katherine Mansfield on E.M. Forster, *diary entry,* May 1917 •870

He is limp and damp and milder than the breath of a cow.

Virginia Woolf on E.M. Forster •871

A village explainer, excellent if you were a village, but if you were not, not. Gertrude Stein on Ezra Pound •872

How unpleasant to meet Mr Eliot!
With his features of clerical cut,
And his brow so grim
And his mouth so prim
And his conversation, so nicely
Restricted to What Precisely
And If and Perhaps and But.

A particularly caustic (but not totally inaccurate) self-assessment from T.S. Eliot, *'Five-Finger Exercises'* (1936) •873

Self-contempt, well-grounded.

F.R. Leavis (1895-1978) on the foundation of T.S. Eliot's work, in *Times Literary Supplement* 21 October 1988 •874

The work of a queasy undergraduate squeezing his pimples. **Virginia Woolf on James Joyce's *Ulysses* ·875**

I am fairly unrepentant about the poetry. I really think that three quarters of its gibberish. However, I must crush down these thoughts, otherwise the dove of peace will shit on me.

Noël Coward on Dame Edith Sitwell ·876

So you've been reviewing Sitwell's last piece of Virgin dung, have you? Isn't she a poisonous thing of a woman, lying, concealing, flipping, plagiarising, misquoting, and being as clever a crooked literary publicist as ever.,

Dylan Thomas on Edith Sitwell ·877

The Sitwells belong to the history of publicity rather than poetry.

FR Leavis in *New Bearings In English Poetry* (1932) ·878

I am reading Proust for the first time. Very poor stuff. I think he was mentally defective.

Evelyn Waugh on Marcel Proust, in *a letter to John Betjemn,* 1948; in *Letters of Evelyn Waugh* (1980) ·879

Miss Stein sometimes takes time from praising Miss Stein to drop names. Vast quantities of names. It's name-dropping because she rarely has anything worthwhile to say about the people attached to them, although they were often the people that did make a difference. *Good-Books-Bad-Books.com* on Gertrude Stein's *The Autobiography of Alice B.Toklas* ·880

I am only one, only one, only one. Only one being, one at the same time. Not two, not three, only one. Only one life to live, only sixty minutes in one hour. Only one pair of eyes. Only one brain. Only one being. Being only one, having only one pair of eyes, having only one time, having only one life, I cannot read your MS three or four times. Not even one time. Only one look, only one look is enough. Hardly one copy would sell here. Hardly one. Hardly one. Many thanks. I am returning the MS by registered post. Only one Ms by one post.

Rejection letter from editor A.J. Fifield to Gertrude Stein, who was renowned (or notorious) for her uniquely repetitive style. ·881

Lady Chatterley's Lover — *Mr Lawrence has a diseased mind. He is obsessed by sex and we have no doubt that he will be ostracised by all except the most degenerate coteries of the world.* John Bull magazine, 1928 ·882

Mr Lawrence looked like a plaster gnome on a stone toadstool in some suburban garden… he looked as if he had just returned from spending an uncomfortable night in a very dark cave. Dame Edith Sit well, on D.H. Lawrence ·883

He has never been known to use a word that might send a reader to the dictionary.

William Faulkner on Ernest Hemingway ·884

Poor Faulkner. Does he really think big emotions come from big words?

Ernest Hemingway on William Faulkner ·885

*[**The Sun Also Rises** is about] bullfighting, bullslinging, and bull****.*

Zelda Fitzgerald offers a summary of Ernest Hemingway's novel; in Marion Meade, *What Fresh Hell Is This?* (1988) ·886

English literature's performing flea.

Sean O'Casey on P.G. Wodehouse ·887

His style has the desperate jauntiness of an orchestra fiddling away for dear life on a sinking ship. Edmund Wilson on Evelyn Waugh ·888

Virginia Woolf's writing is no more than glamorous knitting. I believe she must have a pattern somewhere.

Dame Edith Sitwell ·889

Everything he touches smells like a billygoat. He is every kind of a writer I detest, a faux naif, a Proust in greasy overalls. Raymond Chandler on James M. Cain ·890

Personally, I would rather have written Winnie-the-Pooh than the collected works of Brecht.

Tom Stoppard, attrib. 1972 ·891

The high-water mark, so to speak, of Socialist literature is W.H. Auden, a sort of gutless Kipling.
George Orwell, *The Road to Wigan Pier* (1937) ·892

He is not really a writer, but a non-stop talker to whom someone has given a typewriter.

Gerald Brenan on Henry Miller;
in *Thoughts in a Dry Season* (1978) ·893

After A.A. Milne had written a letter to the Daily Telegraph on the report of Wodehouse's broadcasting from Germany:
My personal animosity against a writer never affects my opinion of what he writes. Nobody could be more anxious than myself, for instance, that Alan Alexander Milne should trip over a loose bootlace and break his bloody neck, yet I re-read his early stuff at regular intervals with all the old enjoyment.

P.G. Wodehouse, *letter,*
27 November 1945 ·894

Oh really. What exactly is she reading?

Actress Dame Edith Evans, on being told that Nancy Mitford had been lent a villa to enable her to finish a book; attrib. ·895

The insolent little ruffian, that Crapulous lout. When he quitted a sofa, he left behind him a smear.

Norman Cameron on Dylan Thomas ·896

To see him fumbling with our rich and delicate language is to experience all the horror of seeing a Sèvres vase in the hands of a chimpanzee.

Evelyn Waugh on Stephen Spender, in *The Tablet*, May 1951 ·897

He is able to turn an unplotted, unworkable manuscript into an unplotted and unworkable manuscript with a lot of sex. **Tom Volpe on Harold Robbins** ·898

*When it comes down to it, **Lucky Jim** is **Just William**, bigger and bespectacled, literate and funny, but scarcely grown-up.*

Simon Gray on Kingsley Amis' *Lucky Jim*, in *The Times* February 1966 ·899

Howl is meant to be a noun, but I can't help taking it as an imperative. **John Hollander on *Howl* by Allan Ginsberg in *The Partisan Review*** ·900

*No, I don't think **Lolita** any good except as smut. As that it was highly exciting to me.*

Evelyn Waugh on Vladimir Nabokov's *Lolita*, in *a letter to Nancy Mitford*, 29 June 1959; **in *Letters of Evelyn Waugh*** (1980) ·901

The trouble with Ian Fleming is that he gets off with women because he can't get on with them.

English novelist Rosamund Lehmann borrows a line from Elizabeth Bowen in her assessment of the James Bond author; in J. Pearson, *The Life of Ian Fleming* (1966) ·902

Good career move.

Gore Vidal, of Truman Capote's death; attrib. ·903

A man who so much resembled a Baked Alaska — sweet, warm and gungy on the outside, hard and cold within. Francis King, of English novelist and scientist C.P. Snow; *Yesterday Came Suddenly* (1993) ·904

I would rather read a novel about civil servants written by a rabbit.

Craig Brown, on hearing that Richard Adams' *Watership Down* was a novel about rabbits written by a civil servant; attrib. ·905

*This is one of those big, fat paperbacks,
intended to while away a monsoon or two,
which, if thrown with a good over-arm action,
will bring a water buffalo to its knees.*

Nancy Banks-Smith, review of M.M. Kaye's *The Far Pavilions* ·906

*Ms. Greer's most succinct descriptive writing is in the title
of her book, which characterises the text with precision.*

Brigid Brophy on Germaine Greer's *The Obstacle Race;* in
London Review of Books, November 1979 ·907

To a Hollywood writer who had criticised the work of Alan Bennett: Listen, dear, you couldn't write fuck on a dusty venetian blind.

English actress Coral Browne; attib., in *Sunday Times Magazine* 1984 ·908

He was not a serious politician.
But his footwork should command
respect. He is proof of the proposition
that in each of us lurks one bad novel.

Julian Critchley on Jeffrey Archer •909

The meringue–utan.

Maurice Bowra (1898-1971), of author Rosamund Lehmann, in *The Spectator* July 1999 •910

I am as shallow as a puddle.

Helen Fielding, creator of *Bridget Jones* •911

The covers of this book are too far apart.

Ambrose Bierce, *review* ·912

POISONED PENS

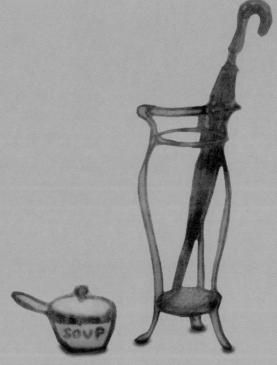

*Heaven sends us good meat,
but the Devil sends cooks.*

David Garrick, *On Doctor Goldsmith's Characteristical Cookery* (1777) ·913

They make a rare soop they call Pepper-Pot; it's an excellent Breakfast for a Salamander, or a good preparative for a Mountebank's Agent, who Eats Fire one day, that he may get better Victual the next. Three Spoonfuls so Inflam'd my Mouth, that had I devoured a Peck of Horse-Radish, and Drank after it a Gallon of Brandy and Gunpowder, I could not have been more importunate for a Drop of Water to cool my Tongue. **Edward Ward** ·914

When I ask for a watercress sandwich, I do not mean a loaf with a field in the middle of it. **Oscar Wilde to a waiter, recorded by Max Beerbohm in a *letter to Reggie Turner*,** 4 February 2002 ·915

There are twenty ways of cooking a potato, and three hundred and sixty-four ways of cooking an egg, yet the British cook up to the present moment knows only three methods of sending up either one or the other.

Oscar Wilde, *'Dinners and Dishes'* (1885) ·916

The average cooking in the average English hotel for the average Englishman explains to a large extent the English bleakness and taciturnity. Nobody can beam and warble while chewing pressed beef smeared with daibolical mustard. Nobody can exult aloud while ungluing from his teeth a quivering tapioca pudding. **Karel Capek** ·917

Nothing but joints, joints, joints; sometimes, perhaps, a meat-pie, which, if you eat it, weighs upon your conscience, with the idea that you have eaten the scraps of other people's dinners. **Nathaniel Hawthorne on food served in English hotels ·918**

The food we ate was risibly bad, the atmosphere smilingly inhospitable, the décor a sordid cliché of rural nostalgia, puppy porn and green-welly fascism — and they charge you two quid to sit on the ground outside. It is not just everything I despise and loath in lunch, but everything that embarrasses and depresses me about tweedy Albion. **The Bell at Sapperton in Gloucestershire gets the AA Gill treatment ·919**

Her cooking is the missionary position of cooking. That is how everybody starts.

Egon Ronay defends Delia Smith (and damns her with faint praise?); in *Independent on Sunday,* November 1998 ·920

Anchovies: I met my first anchovy on a pizza in 1962, and it was seven years before I mustered the courage to go near another. I am known to cross a street whenever I see an anchovy coming. Why would anybody consciously choose to eat a tiny, oil-soaked, leathery maroon strip of rank and briny flesh

Jeffrey Steingarten on *My food phobias,* in his introduction to *The Man Who Ate Everything* (1997) ·921

The anchovy starter was the worst thing I've eaten since I inadvertently swallowed a large flying insect while laughing open-mouthed in Greece. **Sue Townsend ·922**

*Mass-produced food, poor service, and a cold atmosphere —
brickbats abound for the cavernous relaunched Liverpool Street
hotel dining room which has London's leading restaurant name
behind it — Conran c**p at Conran prices, as one reviewer
succinctly put it.* Report on Aurora, in **Harden's London Restaurants 2001** ·923

*Nobu-lite is taking over the eating-out world. It's not McDonald's that's
the real sin of exploitative globalisation, it's this no-no-Nobu non-food.
Sushi-size me? Frankly, I'd rather eat with the fishes.* AA Gill on
Sumosan ·924

*The name Big Mac is generally supposed to have
come about because it is a big McDonald's burger,
but in fact it was named after the big raincoat whose
taste it so closely resembles.* Jo Brand ·925

*It was like chewing a vasectomy scar
with a pustular, yellow skin — as
nasty a burger as I've eaten this year.*

AA Gill on the fayre at The Barnes Grill ·926

*Clams: I feel a mild horror about what goes on in the wet darkness between the
shells of all bivalves, but clams are the only ones I dislike. Is it their rubbery
consistency or their rank subterranean taste, or is the horror deeper than I know?*
Jeffrey Steingarten on **My food phobias,** in his introduction to **The Man Who Ate Everything** (1997) ·927

Turbot, Sir, said the waiter, placing before me two fishbones, two eyeballs, and a bit of a black mackintosh.

Thomas Earle Welby, in *The Dinner Knell* (1932) ***'Birmingham or Crewe?'*** ·928

Adults who require a salad at every meal are like obsessed little children who will eat nothing but frozen pizza or canned ravioli for months on end. They tuck into the dreariest salad simply because it is raw and green. No matter that the arugula is edged with brown, the croutons taste rancid, the vinegar burns like battery acid. No matter that it is the dead of winter when salad chills us to the marrow and we should be eating preserved meats and hearty roots, garbures, and cassoulet. No matter that they are keeping me from my desert. They think nothing of interrupting a perfectly nice meal with their superstitious salad ritual. **Jeffrey Steingarten in *The Man Who Ate Everything*** (1997) ·929

The catering trade is laughingly called the hospitality industry. That's a joke. Any less hospitable industry would be hard to find. The frequent receptionist greeting "Have you got a reservation?" typifies the arrogance of many restaurants… How many times are you greeted in a restaurant with a smile? A smile to most restaurant employees is like a silver cross to a vampire.

Michael Winner, in his introduction to *Winner's Dinners* (2000) ·930

Conran complacency shines through at this noisy and cavernous Soho tourist-trap; surly service and slapdash cooking too often make it a waste of time and money.

Report on Mezzo, in *Harden's London Restaurants* 2002 ·931

The food at Jaan is, by turns stupid, ill thought-out, or just plain nasty. I may not be able to call it the worst cooking in Britain, but that's only because I haven't eaten in every restaurant in the land. Why am I being so harsh? Because a meal here with wine will set you back £65 a head. You do not spend this sort of money so that chefs can do ludicrous things to food.

Jay Rayner in *The Observer* ·932

> *The soup, thin and dark and utterly savourless, tasted as if it had been drained out of the umbrella stand.* **Margaret Halsey on English cuisine** ·933

None of Liebrandt's peculiar touches, however, prepared me for the outlandish goofiness of the desserts. The creations are mostly ethereal flans, foams, and gelées made with ingredients like Pepsi, mentholyptus, or Guinness stout. The Guinness is served in jellied form, as part of a tasteless flan made with orange water; the Pepsi is reduced down, then dripped over a kind of frothy, whiskey-flavoured zabaglione. I'm not sure either of them tasted very good, but then, that's not always the point at Papillon. Spectacle is the point, and in the end, you can't help enjoying the show. **Adam Platt on Papillon in *New York Magazine,*** February 2002 ·934

I was distracted by my friend's filet mignon sandwich. Could I trust a steakhouse that serves a flavourless cut like filet mignon as its special? Dessert answered that. A single scoop of tangerine sorbet arrived in a giant round bowl. I peered in, and it reminded me of a pebble at the bottom of a well.

It made me think of what Tim Zagat, a founder of Restaurant Week, said. It's in the interest of the restaurant to do it well, he said. If the restaurant goes cheap, the restaurant is just damaging its own image.

Indeed. Next time, I'll buy a hot dog and take in the view from the terminal steps. **Amanda Hesser on Michael Jordan's: The Steak House in Grand Central Terminus. In *The New York Times,*** February 2002 ·935

Duck magret, a cut which has become a cliché — and which often isn't magret (the fattened breast of a foie gras bird) but something puny in an A cup.

Jonathan Meades in the
Times Saturday Review,
March 1994 •936

The menu at the Café du Jardin translates poulet provençal as brick flattened chicken, which sounds like a terrible thing to happen to a fowl — the result of a tragic hod incident on La Canebiere, perhaps.

This is not the only solecism on show. The two doors to the street are constantly left open, causing the customer who has drawn the short seat to get up time and again to fight back the draught. The staff are on the diffident side. The tables are so cramped that intimacy could occur, Constable. Jonathan Meades in the
Times Saturday Review,
March 1994 •937

I never liked beer. It's plebeian. It goes with dirty undershirts.
Hedy Lamarr •938

It has, with great panache, expense and devil-take-the-hindmost braggadocio, transformed itself into the most laughably hideous dining room in London. No, credit where credit's due, this is no time to be mealy-mouthed or damn with faint insult — why should only London bask in its horrendous radiance? It's the worst dining room in Britain, in Europe, the globe, the galaxy, history, eternity, ever.
AA Gill on the Dorchester Grill •939

Be content to remember that those who can make omlettes properly can do nothing else.

Hilaire Belloc, *A Conversation with a Cat* (1931) ·940

THE GREAT WITS

When a gentleman is disposed to swear, it is not for any standers-by to curtail his oaths.

William Shakespeare, *Cymbeline* (1609-10) I.vi ·941

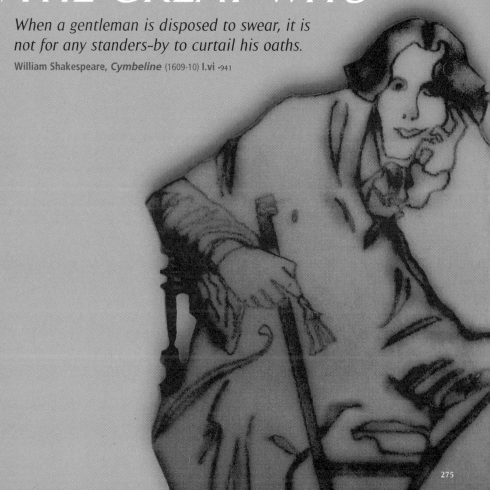

The devil damn thee black, thou cream-faced loon!

William Shakespeare, *Macbeth*, V,iii ·942

A joyless, dismal, black, and sorrowful issue: Here is the babe as loathsome as a toad amongst the fairest breeders of our clime

William Shakespeare, *Titus Andronicus* (1594) iV, ii ·943

What I think I utter, and spend my malice in my breath.

William Shakespeare, *Coriolanus* (1608) II.i ·944

I would thou didst itch from head to foot and I had the scratching of thee.

William Shakespeare, *Troilus and Cressida* (1602) II.i ·945

Beatrice: *I wonder that you will still be talking,*
Signior Benedick: *Nobody marks you. Benedick What!*
  My dear Lady Disdain, are you yet living?

William Shakespeare, *Much Ado About Nothing* (1598-99) I.i ·946

I will go on the slightest errand now to the Antipodes that you can devise to send me on; I will fetch you a toothpicker now from the furthest inch of Asia; bring you the length of Prester John's foot; fetch you a hair of the Great Cham's beard; do you any embassage to the Pigmies, rather than hold three words conference with this harpy.

William Shakespeare, *Much Ado About Nothing* (1598-99) II.i ·947

I do desire we may be better strangers.

William Shakespeare, *As You Like It* (1599) III.ii ·948

*She speaks poniards, and every word stabs:
if her breath were as terrible as her
terminations, there were no living near
her; she would infect to the north star.*

William Shakespeare, *Much Ado About Nothing* (1598-9) II.i ·949

Thou subtle, perjur'd, false, disloyal man!

William Shakespeare, *The Two Gentlemen of Verona* (1592-3) IV.ii ·950

*I do defy him, and spit at him;
Call him a slanderous coward
and a villain.* William Shakespeare, *Richard II* (1595) I.i ·951

Vile worm, thou wast o'er looked even in thy birth

William Shakespeare, *The Merry Wives Of Windsor*(1597) **V.v** •952

A most notable coward, an infinite and endless liar, an hourly promise breaker, the owner of no one good quality worthy your Lordship's entertainment

William Shakespeare, *All's Well That Ends Well* (1603-4) **III.vi** •953

Poor virgin, sir, an ill-favoured thing, sir, but mine own; a poor humour of mine, sir, to take that that no man else will.

William Shakespeare, *As you Like It* (1599-1600) **V.iv** •954

*That trunk of humours, that
bolting-hutch of beastliness,
that swollen parcel of dropsies,
that huge bombard of sack,
that stuffed cloak-bag of
guts, that roasted Manningtree
ox with pudding in his belly,
that reverend vice, that grey
iniquity, that father ruffian,
that vanity in years.*

**William Shakespeare,
Henry IV, Part 1** (1597) II.iv •955

*'sblood, you starvelling,
you eel-skin, you dried
neat's-tongue, you
bull's pizzle, you
stock-fish — O for
breath to utter what
is like thee!- you
tailor's-yard, you
sheath, you bow-case,
you vile standing tuck!*

William Shakespeare, Henry IV, Part 1
(1597) II.iv •956

Thou art a traitor and a miscreant,
too good to be so and too bad to live.

William Shakespeare, *Richard II* (1595) I.i ·957

'zounds, a dog, a rat, a mouse, a cat, to scratch a man to
death! A braggart, a rogue, a villain, that fights by the
book of arithmetic! William Shakespeare, *Romeo And Juliet* (1595)III.i ·958

O! he's as tedious
As a tired horse, a railing wife;
Worse than a smoky house. I had rather live
With cheese and garlic in a windmill, far,
Than feed on cates and have him talk to me
In any summer-house in Christendom.

William Shakespeare, *Henry IV, Part 1* (1597) III.i ·959

Away you scullion! You rampallion!
You fustilarian! I'll tickle
your catastophe!

William Shakespeare,
Henry IV, Part 2 (1597) II.i ·960

Why, he is the prince's jester: a very dull fool;
Only his gift is in devising impossible slanders:
None but libertines delight in him;
And the
Commendation is not in his wit, but in his villainy

William Shakespeare, *Much Ado About Nothing* (1598-9) II.i ·961

Thou clay-brained guts,
thou knotty-pated fool,
thou whoreson obscene
greasy tallow-catch!

William Shakespeare, *Henry IV, Part 1* (1597) II.iv ·962

Johnson: *Well, we had a good talk.*
Boswell: *Yes, sir, you tossed and gored several persons.*

Boswell's account of a post-prandial exchange between Johnson and himself ·963

Nay, sir, we'll send you to him. If your presence doesn't drive a man out of his house, nothing will.

Samuel Johnson to James Boswell, discussing how to get a friend to leave London ·964

Sir, there is no settling the point of precedency between a louse and a flea.

Samuel Johnson on the relative merits of two minor poets; in James Boswell, *Life of Samuel Johnson* (1791) 1783 ·965

This man I thought had been a Lord among wits; but, I find, he is only a wit among Lords.

Samuel Johnson on Lord Chesterfield; in James Boswell, *Life of Samuel Johnson* (1791) 1754 ·966

Sir, he was dull in company, dull in his chest, dull everywhere. He was dull in a new way, and that made many people think him great. He was a mechanical poet. Samuel Johnson on Thomas Gray ·967

Young man: *Tell me this, Sir, what would you give to be as young and sprightly as I am?*
Johnson: *Why, Sir, I should almost be content to be as foolish and conceited.*

Samuel Johnson; in Kenneth Williams, *Acid Drops* (1980) ·968

Johnson: *Sir, it is a very vile country.*
Mr S—: *Well, Sir, God made it.*
Johnson: *Certainly he did, but we must remember that He made it for Scotchmen; and comparisons are odious, Mr. S—, but God made Hell.*

Samuel Johnson on Scotland ·969

Oats. A grain, which in England is generally given to horses but in Scotland supports the people.

Samuel Johnson, *Dictionary of the English Language* ·970

Difficult do you call it, Sir? I wish it were impossible.

Samuel Johnson, on the performance of a celebrated violinist, in William Seward, *Supplement to the Anecdotes of Distinguished Persons* (1797) ·971

***Paradise Lost** is one of those books which the readers admires, lays down and forgets to take up again. Its perusal is a duty rather than a pleasure.*

Samuel Johnson ·972

I refute it thus.

Samuel Johnson, kicking a large stone by way of refuting Bishop Berkeley's theory of the non-existence of matter, in Boswell, *Life of Samuel Johnson* (1791) *6 August 1763* ·973

A fellow who makes no figure in company, and has a mind as narrow as the neck of a vinegar cruet.

Samuel Johnson, in Boswell, *Journal of a Tour in the Hebrides* (1785) ·974

I do not want people to be very agreeable, as it saves me the trouble of liking them a great deal.

Jane Austen, *letter to her sister Cassandra,* 24-6 December 1798 •975

Mrs Breton called here on Saturday. I never saw her before. She is large, ungenteel woman, with self-satisfied and would-be elegant manners.

Jane Austen, *Letter to her sister Cassandra* •976

A person and face, of strong, natural, sterling insignificance.

Jane Austen, *Sense and Sensibility* (1811) •977

I cannot anyhow continue to find people agreeable; I respect Mrs Chamberlayne for doing her hair well, but cannot feel a more tender sentiment. Miss Langley is like any other short girl, with a broad nose and wide mouth, fashionable dress and exposed bosom. Adam Stanhope is a gentleman-like man, but then his legs are too short and his tail too long.

Jane Austen, *Letter to her sister Cassandra* •978

'My love, you contradict every body,' said his wife with her usual laugh. 'Do you know that you are quite rude?'
'I did not know I contradicted anybody in calling your mother ill-bred.' **Jane Austen,** *Sense and Sensibility* (1811) •979

Mrs Hall of Sherbourne was brought to bed yesterday of a dead child, some weeks before she expected, owing to a fright. I suppose she happened to look unawares at her husband.

Jane Austen, *letter* •980

Miss Debary, Susan and Sally... made their appearance, and I was as civil to them as their bad breath would allow me.

Jane Austen, *letter to Cassandra,* 11 June 1799 •981

It was a delightful visit; — perfect, in being much too short.

Jane Austen, *Emma* (1816) •982

It is perfectly monstrous the way people go about nowadays, saying things against one behind one's back that are absolutely true.

Oscar Wilde, *The Picture of Dorian Gray* (1891) ·983

He hasn't an enemy in the world, and none of his friends like him.

Oscar Wilde on George Bernard Shaw ·984

One must have a heart of stone to read the death of Little Nell without laughing.

Oscar Wilde on Charles Dickens' *Little Dorrit* ·985

Mr. Henry James writes fiction as it were a painful duty.

Oscar Wilde ·986

I hate vulgar realism in literature. The man who would call a spade a spade should be compelled to use one. It is the only thing he is fit for.

Oscar Wilde, *The Picture of Dorian Gray* (1891) ·987

Gwendolen: I had no idea there were any flowers in the country.
Cecily: Oh, flowers are as common here, Miss Fairfax, as people are in London.
Oscar Wilde, *The Importance of Being Earnest* (1895) *Act III* ·988

Miss Prism: No married man is ever attractive except to his wife.
Chasuble: And often, I've been told, not even to her.
Oscar Wilde, *The Importance of Being Earnest* (1895) *Act II* ·989

…Lady Ruxton, an overdressed woman of forty-seven, with a hooked nose, who was always trying to get herself compromised, but was so peculiarly plain that to her great disappointment no one would ever believe anything against her.
Oscar Wilde, *The Picture of Dorian Gray* (1891) ·990

Thy body is hideous. It is like the body of a leper. It is like a plastered wall where vipers have crawled.
Oscar Wilde, *Salomé* (1894) ·991

…A dowdy girl, with one of those characteristic British faces, that, once seen are never remembered.
Oscar Wilde, *The Picture of Dorian Gray* (1891) ·992

And now you must run away, for I am dining with some very dull people, who won't talk scandal, and I know that if I don't get my sleep now I shall never be able to keep awake during dinner.

Oscar Wilde, **Lord Arthur Savile's Crime** (1891) •993

Unable to accept due to a subsequent engagement.

Oscar Wilde responds to a dinner invitation; attrib., perhaps apocryphal,
in Kenneth Williams, **Acid Drops** (1980) •994

Relations are simply a tedious pack of people, who haven't got the remotest knowledge of how to live, nor the smallest instinct about when to die.

Oscar Wilde, **The Importance of Being Earnest** (1895) *Act I* •995

Of course, America had been discovered before Columbus, but it had always been hushed up.

Oscar Wilde •996

It is absurd to say that there are neither ruins nor curiosities in America when they have their mothers and their manners.

Oscar Wilde •997

Wilde: How I wish I had said that. James McNeill Whistler: You will, Oscar, you will.

In R. Ellman, **Oscar Wilde** (1987) •998

Under certain circumstances, profanity provides a relief denied even to prayer. Mark Twain •999

Better to keep your mouth shut and appear stupid than to open it and remove all doubt.

Mark Twain; James Munson (ed.) *The Sayings of Mark Twain* (1992); attrib., perhaps apocryphal. Twain's advice was later dispensed by Norman Tebbit to Dennis Skinner •1000

A solemn, unsmiling, sanctimonious old iceberg that looked like he was waiting for a vacancy on the Trinity.

Mark Twain, of a California leader in the 1960s, later taken up by H.L. Mencken and applied to Woodrow Wilson; in Alex Ayres (ed.), *The Wit and Wisdom of Mark Twain* (2005) •1001

Suppose you were an idiot. And suppose you were a member of Congress. But I repeat myself.

Mark Twain; in Alex Ayres (ed.), *The Wit and Wisdom of Mark Twain* (2005) •1002

Let his vices be forgotten and his virtues remembered; it will not infringe much upon any man's time.

Mark Twain; in Alex Ayres (ed.), *The Wit and Wisdom of Mark Twain* (2005) •1003

I refused to attend his funeral, but I wrote a very nice letter explaining that I approved of it.

Mark Twain, on hearing of the death of a corrupt politician; in James Munson (ed.) *The Sayings of Mark Twain* (1992) •1004

That woman speaks eighteen langauges, and can't say 'No' in any of them.

Dorothy Parker; in Alexander Woollcott, *While Rome Burns* (1934) ·1005

If all the girls attending it were laid end to end, I wouldn't be at all surprised.

Dorothy Parker, of the Yale Prom, recalled in Alexander Woollcott, ***While Rome Burns*** (1934) ·1006

You can lead a horticulture, but you can't make her think.

Dorothy Parker ·1007

Clare Booth Luce (meeting Dorothy Parker in a doorway): Age before beauty.
Parker (proceeding through the doorway): Pearls before swine.

In R.E. Drennan, *Wit's End* (1973) ·1008

And where does she find them?

Dorothy Parker, on hearing that Clare Booth Luce was always kind to her inferiors; in Marion Meade, ***What Fresh Hell is This?*** (1988) ·1009

Nobody has any business to go around looking like horse and behaving as if it were all right. You don't catch horses going around looking like people do you? Dorothy Parker ·1010

She wore a low but futile décolletage.
Dorothy Parker ·1011

You mean those clothes of hers are intentional?
Dorothy Parker ·1012

As a source of entertainment, conviviality and good fun, she ranks somewhere between a sprig of parsley and a single ice-skate.
Dorothy Parker ·1013

Now to me, Edith looks like something that would eat her young. Dorothy Parker on Edith Evans, British stage and screen actress ·1014

She has only two expressions — joy and indigestion.
Dorothy Parker on film star Marion Davies ·1015

In fact, now that you've got me right down to it, the only thing I didn't like about 'The Barretts of Wimpole Street' was the play.
Dorothy Parker in **The New Yorker,** 1931 ·1016

*Its hero is caused, by a novel device, to fall asleep
and a-dream; and thus he is given yesterday. Me,
I should have given him twenty years to life.*

Dorothy Parker on A.A. Milne's play *Give Me Yesterday,* in *The New Yorker,* 1931 •1017

*This is not a novel to be
tossed aside lightly. It should
be thrown with great force.*

Dorothy Parker, in R.E. Drennan, *Wit's End* •1018

*Theodore Dreiser
Should ought to write nicer.*

Dorothy Parker reviewing *Dawn* by Dreiser, in *The New Yorker,* May 1931 •1019

And it is that word hummy, my darlings, that marks the first place in The House at Pooh Corner at which the Tonstant Weader Fwowed up.

Dorothy Parker — under the pseudonym Constant Reader — is nauseated by Pooh's hums in A.A. Milne's *The House at Pooh Corner*. In *The New Yorker*, October 1928 •1020

The affair between Margot Asquith and Margot Asquith will live as one of the prettiest love stories in all literature.

Dorothy Parker reviews Margot Asquith's *Lay Sermons;* in *New Yorker* 22 October 1927 •1021

*If, with the literate, I am
Impelled to try an epigram,
I never seek to take the credit;
We all assume that Oscar said it.*

Dorothy Parker, 'A Pig's-Eye View of Literature' (1937) ·1022

*I'm just a little Jewish girl
trying to be cute.*

If you say so, Dorothy ·1023

How can they tell?

Dorothy Parker, on being informed that
Calvin Coolidge was dead ·1024

THANKS TO

Ayres, Alex (ed.),
The Wit and Wisdom of Mark Twain
(Perennial, 2005)

Bierce, Ambrose & Bufe, Chaz,
*The Devil's Dictionaries: The Best of The Devil's Dictionary and
The American Heretic's Dictionary* (2nd ed.)
(Tucson, AZ: See Sharp Press, 2004)

Blackadder: The Whole Damn Dynasty 1485-1917
(London: Penguin, 1999)

Enright, Dominique (compiler)
The Wicked Wit of Jane Austen
(London: Michael O'Mara Books, 2002)

Enright, Dominique (compiler)
The Wicked Wit of Winston Churchill
(London: Michael O'Mara Books, 2001)

Hill, Wayne F. & Öttchen, Cynthia J. (ed.)
Shakespeare's Insults: Educating Your Wit
(London: Ebury Press, 2006)

Kemp, Peter (ed.)
The Oxford Dictionary of Literary Quotations
(Oxford: Oxford University Press, 1997)

Knight, Gred (ed.),
The Past Times Book of Right Honourable Insults
(Past Times, 1998)

Knowles, Elizabeth (ed.),
The Oxford Dictionary of Phrase, Saying and Quotation
(Oxford: Oxford University Press, 1997)

Jarski, Rosemarie (ed.),
The Funniest Things You Never Said
(London: Ebury Press, 2004)

Leach, Maria (compiler),
The Wicked Wit of Oscar Wilde
(London: Michael O'Mara Books, 2000)

Lovric, Michelle,
Women's Wicked Wit: From Jane Austen to Roseanne Barr
(London: Prion Books, 2000)

Lynn, Jonathan & Jay, Antony,
The Complete Yes Minister
(London: BBC Books, 1984)

McPhee, Nancy,
The Complete Book of Insults
(BCA, 1995)

Ostow, Micol & Brezenoff, Steven (ed.),
The Quotable Slayer
(London: Pocket Books, 2003)

Parris, Matthew (ed.),
Scorn: With Extra Bile
(London: Penguin, 1998)

The Times Book of Quotations
(Glasgow: Times Books, 2000)

Ward, Laura (ed.), *Bad Press:
The Worst Critical Reviews Ever*
(London: PRC Publishing, 2002)

Williams, Kenneth,
Acid Drops
(London: Coronet, 1981)

Various websites including the excellent *www.wikiquote.org*

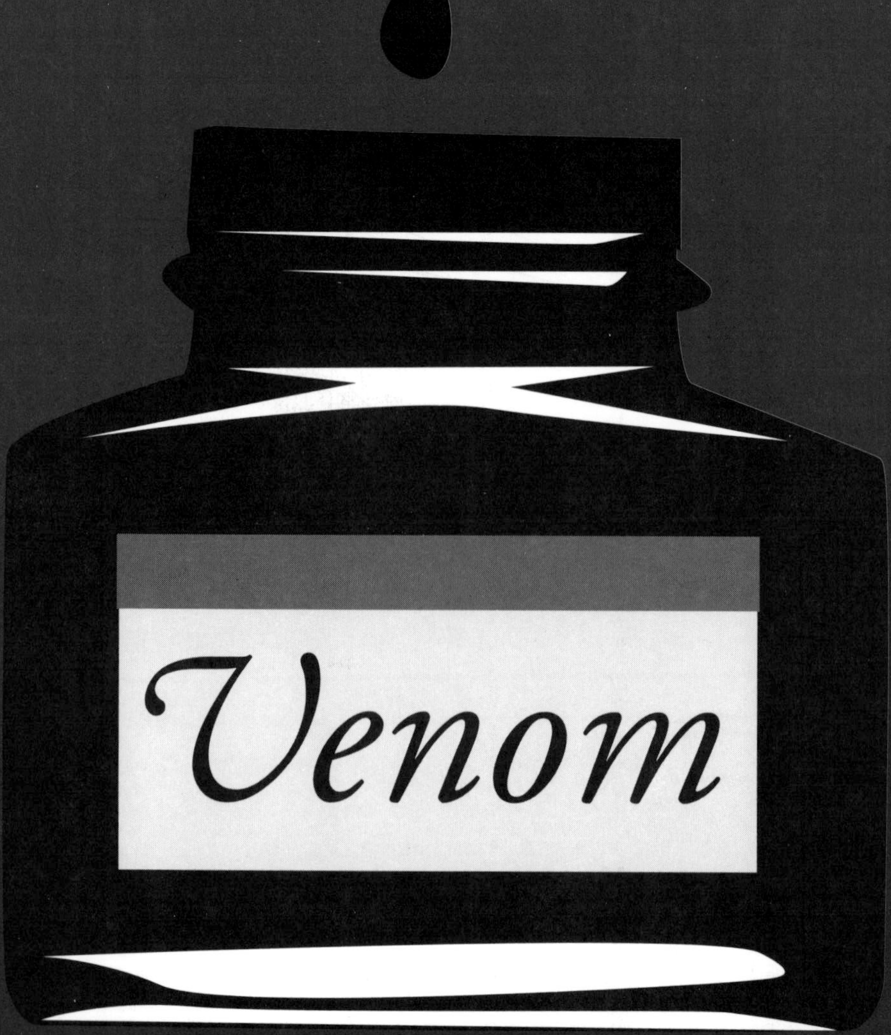
Venom